ALBUQUERQUE

A CELEBRATION OF CONTRASTS

WRITTEN BY GREGOR KRAUSE
PHOTOGRAPHY BY JERRY RABINOWITZ*
ART DIRECTION BY BECKY WAGLEY, WAGLEY DESIGN
CORPORATE PROFILES BY MICHAEL BAWAYA
*(EXCEPT AS NOTED)

COPYRIGHT 1996 STARLIGHT PUBLISHING
LYNDELL F. GOOCH, PRESIDENT · RICK HOMANS, CHAIRMAN

STARLIGHT PUBLISHING, 600 FIRST ST. NW, ALBUQUERQUE, NM 87102. 505-768-7008
ISBN: 0-9648199-0-2

ALBUQUERQUE

A CELEBRATION OF CONTRASTS

STARLIGHT PUBLISHING, INC.
PUBLISHED IN COOPERATION WITH THE GREATER ALBUQUERQUE CHAMBER OF COMMERCE

C O N T E N T S

TITLE PAGE PICTURES

TOP ROW: Linda Cotton, Park Square I and II. **SECOND ROW:** Matachine dancers, Copper Square (taken from inside),
a traditional carved santo. **THIRD ROW:** The KiMo Theater, First Plaza courtyard, Congregation B'nai Israel synagogue.
FOURTH ROW: Embedded arrow at Indian Plaza shopping center, El Vado Motel, Martineztown mural.

FACING PAGE

The Kodak© Albuquerque International Balloon Fiesta, the city's spectacular signature event, is the largest and most
popular ballooning event in the world.

OVERLEAFS 6-13

6: Nature kindly gifted Albuquerque with the Sandias and the Rio Grande.

8: Bernalillo County Sheriff's Deputy Joe Bruno works with kids—he's with the Drug Awareness Re-Education program—and plays
with them, too—visiting classrooms to sing with them; coaching baseball, basketball, and softball at Valley High School; and establishing real
relationships with them. (Photo by Eric O'Connell)

10: A tight cluster of high-rise structures marks Albuquerque's downtown business district, making for a sharp but appealing contrast to the city's
predominant low-profile, one- and two-story architecture. From the northeast, the commercial center is backdropped by one of the city's great
landmarks, the Rio Grande, which makes a lazy, graceful bend here as it heads south.

12: Albuquerque honors the separate threads of its richly blended heritage in a variety of ways. Every April, it celebrates
Founder's Day in a sprawling event drenched in music, food, performance (including these Hispanic dancers in full-dress finery
performing in Old Town), a parade, and more.

A L B U Q U E R Q U E

ALBUQUERQUE could well be the Great American City.

It is archetypically American— almost a microcosm of the country as a whole—embodying the virtues and ideals on which the nation itself was founded. It is the definition of racial and ethnic diversity, more openly and acceptingly polycultural than virtually any other city in the country. Within its city limits, its constituent communities represent all of the significant eras and phases in the nation's evolution—the rural, the urban, the industrial, the suburban. Albuquerque honors the beauty of the American landscape with a skyline that's not a palisade of modern skyscrapers and towering hotels, but a pair of small mountain ranges that rise suddenly just northeast of the city, offering a stunning series of color and weather changes throughout the year—while also thriving as a modern city that accommodates everything from smokestack industries and a symphony orchestra to shopping malls and superb restaurants. It also combines a deep-rooted past, with human habitation dating back thousands of years, and a visionary future, being home to laboratories leading the nation in both defense technology and conversion, and the world's largest single producer of computer chips.

The city, the seat of Bernalillo County, has always been a favorite of travelers. For generations of drivers it defines the landscape and the cities of the nation's midsection. Its renown reaches back to the 18th century, when the city became a primary stop on the heavily traveled Camino Real ("Royal Road"), the artery of trade, travel, mail, and commerce that extended some 1,500 miles from Mexico City to the remote village of Taos. But it was the 1926 establishment of Route 66 that burned the image of the city indelibly into the minds of the restless and the itchy-footed across America and around the world. Route 66 transformed Albuquerque into a beloved outpost for highway travelers—a haven of diners, motels, gas stations, automobile repair shops and other comforts in the heart of the 2,200 mile journey from Chicago to Los Angeles. Even before it was immortalized in song (*Get Your Kicks on Route 66*) or the TV series of that name, John

Steinbeck both celebrated and deromanticized the highway in his 1939 novel, *The Grapes of Wrath*: "Highway 66 is the main migrant road - the long concrete path across the country, waving gently up and down on the map, from Mississippi to Bakersfield—over the red lands and gray lands, twisting up into the mountains, crossing the Divide and down into the bright and terrible desert....66 is the mother road...the path of people in flight who streamed out, sometimes a single car, sometimes a little caravan."

Albuquerque is definitively American, yes, but it is also wholly its own, unique. In large part, its uniqueness is due to the fact that it has evolved in something approaching geographical isolation. Albuquerque is set almost at the dead center of New Mexico— in area, the fifth-largest state in the

THROUGH THREE CENTURIES, ALBUQUERQUE HAS BEEN A VITAL METROPOLIS AT ONE OF THE NATION'S MOST IMPORTANT CROSSROADS. TODAY, SILHOUETTE SIGNS (RIGHT) ADORNING THE STREETLIGHT STANDARDS ALONG CENTRAL AVENUE THROUGH THE RE-ENERGIZED DOWNTOWN (ABOVE) MEMORIALIZE THE CITY'S ROMANTIC BOOMTOWN HEYDAY AS ONE OF THE MOST POPULAR WAY STATIONS ON WORLD-FAMOUS ROUTE 66.

nation, but with a population constituting less than 1% of the U.S. The region, the high desert of the American Southwest, is spectacularly beautiful, with the rugged Sandia mountains towering in the distance over the winding Rio Grande. But even today, looking out over the vast, stunning expanses of red and yellow desert plain—covered with rugged shrub and grass and tree— it's not hard to see why this was long regarded as extremely forbidding terrain for pioneers.

This isolation, though, has bred in Albuquerque both ingenuity and an extraordinary and deeply endearing lack of self-consciousness. Most other big cities have appropriated bits and pieces of still other big cities—New York's Central Park is mirrored on the opposite coast by San Francisco's Golden Gate Park; Washington, D.C.'s mall evokes the urban design of several European capitals. Albuquerque has borrowed nothing readily recognizable from outside sources. Instead, it has chosen to model itself in many ways on the settlements of the area's indigenous peoples and early inhabitants.

Yes, the Eastern settlers who arrived with the railroad in the 1880s and 1890s brought with them a preference for the bricks, the clapboards, and the peaked roofs of the Midwestern towns they left. But in the 1920s, when Italian-American immigrant and successful local merchant Oreste Bachechi set about showing his appreciation to his community by building the city a world-class movie theater, it was neither Italian nor colonial American styl-

istic influences that showed up in the design. Instead, he sent his architect around New Mexico to peruse the pueblos, the reservations, the heavily Hispanic small towns, and the natural landscape for whatever elements he could glean and incorporate into a striking design. The result, which cost some $150,000 to build and opened in 1927, was the KiMo Theatre. It remains today a unique structure with its buffalo-skull sconces, war-drum chandeliers, beams textured to resemble traditional vigas, and Hispanic and

> *This isolation, though, has bred in Albuquerque both ingenuity and an extraordinary and deeply endearing lack of self-consciousness.*

widely scattered Native American designs and motifs.

This concerted regionalism wasn't simply a matter of style; it had many pragmatic aspects, too. Adobe was desirable, in an area of climatic extremes, for its insulating effects—and was readily available, since it was made with sandy clay from the surrounding desert. And the construction of a city around a central square or plaza was a defensive device borrowed from the Pueblo Indians. The Indians, unique for settling and constructing permanent structures instead of roaming from place to place, had, by the time of European settle-

ment of the area, long experience fending off raids and invasions by nomadic tribes. Albuquerque's location and sprawling layout made it vulnerable to Indian raids, so the settlers began building their houses around a defensible plaza, with home entrances facing the square. In the event of attack, livestock was herded into the plaza and the settlement was defended from the rooftops. In Albuquerque, the central square is now known as Old Town.

The city's uniqueness and ingenuity is apparent, too, in its decentralized development. Albuquerque and Bernalillo County have evolved as a series of distinct neighborhoods and communities. Historically, they were nothing more than a loose coalition of an inchoate hamlet or two and a broad scattering of farms and ranches—a highly optimistic excuse for an ambitious Spanish bureaucrat to decree a villa. But over the three centuries it has now existed, the city, like the county, has done full honor to that polycentric structure, not simply making it work but making it more effective and desirable than the traditional single-center American model. Remarkably, they have done it while being almost immutably bounded on three sides—by Indian pueblos to the north, by the mountains to the east, and by a 52,000-acre military installation to the south.

However, Albuquerque's inner

city, unlike many others, has remained vibrant and its tax base stable due to an annexation policy that has precluded a number of affluent suburbs emerging and depleting the urban center of residents and revenue.

The region is proud of its educational institutions. The Albuquerque Public Schools' district, which numbers more than 87,000 students and serves all of Bernalillo County, is the 26th largest in the country. Albuquerque Technical Vocational Institute has for more than thirty years instilled students with the requisite skills for entering the labor force. The Southwestern Indian Polytechnic Institute offers business, occupational, and general studies curriculums for Native Americans. The University of New Mexico is the state's preeminent institute of higher learning, offering more than 4,000 courses and granting 241 degrees and certificates.

Albuquerque is a big city—133 square miles in area, with a population of more than 400,000 peo-ple, roughly 30 percent of all New Mexico residents. Bernalillo County, with over 500,000 residents, is by far the most populous, though the smallest in area, of the state's 33 counties. Although not officially a county until New Mexico gained statehood in 1912, it traces its roots back to the first quarter of the 19th century. In 1823, two years after winning independence from Spain, Mexico divided its northern landholdings into four *caberceras* (districts), one of which was named Bernalillo. Records from 1849 indicate that the town of Bernalillo, 15 miles north of Albuquerque (and, ironically, now in Sandoval County) was the county seat and home to the circuit court. In 1851, the legislature of the New Mexico Territory moved the seat and the district court across the river and slightly south, to Los Ranchos de Albuquerque, and three years later moved it again, this time right into Albuquerque's Old Town. In 1878, the seat returned to Bernalillo for five years, and was permanently moved to Albuquerque in 1883. Today, a five commissioner board—each commissioner representing a district within the county—oversees a county manager, who in turn oversees some 1,300 people in 25 departments and controls a budget of more than $100 million a year.

The city and the county also contain all the amenities and a fair amount of the sophistication of a much bigger metropolis—an endless variety, a huge range of possibilities and opportunities, a vast array of choices and surprises. Yet it retains the distinct and unmistakable feel of a small town—the friendliness and candor of the people, the sensation of immediate accessibility.

LOOKING EAST AT THE UNIVERSITY OF NEW MEXICO, MONTE VISTA AVENUE, AND CENTRAL AVENUE, CIRCA 1932 (ABOVE LEFT - PHOTO BY THREE HAWKS © 1995 THE ALBUQUERQUE MUSEUM). THE CITY'S SKYLINE (ABOVE) IS DOMINATED BY THE 22-FLOOR ALBUQUERQUE PLAZA AND THE ADJOINING 20-FLOOR HYATT HOTEL.

Both of these impressions spring from the same source—a sense that the place is really more a loosely organized amalgam of smaller communities, almost cities within the city, than it is a single, large, homogenized entity. Throughout its history the city has shown a marked tendency, and a remarkable ability, to deal with diverse elements that arise near it or in its midst—to annex and absorb, or delineate and set off. At the same time, it is almost Lincolnesque in its dedication to preserving its unity.

When the railroad arrived, for example, it shifted the bulk of the city's commercial and business activity a mile or so east from the

plaza, which had once been virtually the entire city and long its heart. The city simply renamed the plaza area Old Town, named the area astride the tracks and around the depot New Town, and genially accepted the bifurcation.

Later residential and commercial developments would—and continue to—have similar effects: a tract is developed with new homes, giving rise to a shopping center built specifically to serve that market. You can see this today in the communities and complexes that have developed around the university, the airport and Kirtland Air Force Base, Nob Hill, Uptown, Downtown, the Northeast Heights, and the North and South valleys.

The city that resulted from such a course of development could have turned into a fractious hodgepodge, with neighborhoods threatening to secede and establish their own police forces, or putting up gates and speed bumps. But Albuquerque has shown exceptional skill in marshaling this

array of factions and neighborhoods—and as a result it is one of the nation's few major cities that still conveys a genuine sense of community.

This gives the city a profoundly enviable air of diversity—diversity in all its parts, diversity in all things. Along its northern edge lies an area of manufacturing plants and warehouse complexes. The corrugated walls and no-nonsense parking lots may not look like much, but this area is home to, among other things, Albuquerque Civic Light Opera Association (the biggest and most successful all-musical community theater in the nation), and the Gruet winery. East of the freeway are the new homes and the luxe apartment complexes of the Northeast Heights, the exclusive Tanoan Country Club communities, and the spectacular multimillion dollar homes in the foothills of the Sandias.

The city's southern sections present a living diorama of Southwestern agricultural history

and a vivid glimpse of the city's long past as a Spanish farming and ranching center. The road passes through lush river valleys on the Indian reservation, brilliant green floors of alfalfa and other crops, then enters the city, which here seems as rural as a Midwestern farm town—cornfields, vegetable gardens, livestock in pens, chickens at back porches, irrigation ditches beside the road, tractors in sideyards, hay barns, dirt streets and driveways.

To the west, the city rises suddenly from the high desert in the form of new housing developments on the West Mesa, their immaculate, emerald lawns and parks ingeniously worked into the landscape, their two-story homes and divided streets a picture-perfect suburban dreamscape. The West Side is growing rapidly and is the site of Albuquerque's newest and largest shopping mall, Cottonwood.

This, one of the newest parts of the city, gives way almost instantly to one of the most historic—the

close, old neighborhoods of adobe homes and walled gardens at the head of the South Valley and the foot of the North Valley. And there is the Rio Grande, a broad expanse of sedate green water with people playing and fishing from the banks and a series of gentle sandbars that step clear around the next bend.

> *The city's southern sections present a living diorama of Southwestern agricultural history and a vivid glimpse of the city's long past as a Spanish farming and ranching center.*

From the east, the traveler passes some of New Mexico's tiniest towns and expanses of broadly scattered homes before entering a surprisingly mountainous landscape—the backside of the Sandias,

the city and county's dogged protector against all but the biggest storms, the highest winds, the fiercest rains and snows. The east side of the range sees considerably more precipitation than the city does, and the landscape becomes lusher and greener the closer you get to the mountains. This sector of the metro area is experiencing phenomenal growth. It still looks so wild and hardscrabble from the highway that it's hard to imagine it's only 15 minutes from Downtown Albuquerque—and that's precisely why commuters are flocking out here looking for bigger lots, cheaper land, and a more rural feel than can be found in the city. This is an area of burgeoning towns that are setting up chambers of commerce in buildings shared with post offices, banks, and ATMs. Around one last curve, the interstate begins dropping fast from the city's high eastern edge into the shallow river valley. Here

there are schools and apartment complexes, close-knit neighborhoods with quiet, curving streets and perfect pocket parks, two of the city's three shopping malls—commercial centers serving shoppers from six states—several of its most popular restaurants, leading hotels, and one of the most successful office complexes in the history of the state.

Albuquerque's predilection for loosely enfolding new elements and entities, instead of laying claim to them, is also apparent in its burgeoning suburbs.

Albuquerque didn't create them, but it has transformed them. Los Lunas, 24 miles south, was part of a 1716 land grant claimed by the Luna family (the town's name means "The Lunas," as in the Luna Family, not "the moons") and turned by them into a sheep ranching and political power center. The family's opulent latter-day mansion, built by the Santa Fe Railroad in the early 1880s as part of a deal for a railroad right-of-way, is now a restaurant. The town lacks an industrial base of any conse-

quence, but it has become a booming residential bedroom community for Albuquerque commuters. Belen, 10 miles farther south than Los Lunas, was another land grant settlement (*Nuestra Señora de Belén*—Our Lady of Bethlehem) of farmers, ranchers, and laborers. Brought dramatically to life in the 1880s with the arrival of the railroad, the city would be today little

> *Albuquerque's predilection for loosely enfolding new elements and entities instead of laying claim to them is also apparent in its burgeoning suburbs.*

more than a quaint (and charming) vestige of the region's past were it not for the easy commute it affords into Albuquerque. Belen, too, is enjoying a housing boom as a bedroom community for the big

city half an hour north.

But the most dramatic case history in the region is that of Rio Rancho, centered about 20 miles northwest of Downtown Albuquerque. In 1961, the American Petroleum and Realty Corporation (AMREP) bought some 55,000 acres of unpromising sagebrush-covered pastureland on a mesa overlooking the Rio Grande. The company, based in New York, began aggressively marketing undeveloped lots in the parcel as sections of a retirement community, but soon shifted strategies and began developing the area as a haven of affordable housing for first-time home buyers, and bolstered the city's appeal by luring employers as well. The

effort soon proved successful enough to spawn a new subsidiary company—AMREP Southwest—to manage Rio Rancho's phenomenal growth. Rio Rancho now spreads from the high-density suburban developments on the west bank of the Rio Grande to sprawling homes with golf course frontages and breathtaking views across Albuquerque to the mountains. Initially viable due only to its proximity to Albuquerque, Rio Rancho is now the fastest growing micropolitan area in the nation, and is projected to become the second-largest city in New Mexico (behind Albuquerque) within the next 15 years. It is a seat of high-tech industry—home to Intel's largest production facility, a manufacturing division of Intuit (maker of, among other products, Quicken©), and others. And it has become a crucial engine driving the region's economy.

By virtually every meaningful measure, the quality of life in Albuquerque and Bernalillo County equals or surpasses that available in any other major metropolis in this country. There is more open space and a more resolute approach to preserving it than in many other metro areas. There is a richer system of ethnic cultures in linked communities—

but nothing like the ghettos that crop up in other major cities. There are lots of Asian restaurants, a handful of authentic markets, and a sizable Asian population, but no Chinatown, no Little Tokyo. There are dozens of Italian restaurants and thousands of Italians, but no Little Italy. The population is roughly 37% Hispanic, but there's no Olvera Street. The elements come together here, and, as hackneyed as it may sound, the city and the county serve as a great melting pot.

> *In the firmament of American metropolitan areas, this is one of the brightest stars in the brightest constellation.*

Albuquerque's not Los Angeles or San Francisco or New York in terms of traditional high culture, though it does boast a symphony orchestra held in high esteem not only regionally but nationally. But the city is immersed in a centuries-old artisan tradition that makes it a haven for artists and craftspeople like no other in this country.

In the firmament of American metropolitan areas, this is one of the brightest stars in the brightest constellation.

So why, you may reasonably wonder, do you not hear more about it? Why is it so difficult, as it were, to see it with the naked eye?

For one thing, it is smaller than the other major metropolitan areas

of the American Southwest. Within the five-state region, it has the 11th largest population.

For another, its highly self-reliant development doesn't give the visitor, the resident, the critic, or even the hagiographer many easy points of reference. It has no Gateway Arch, no Golden Gate Bridge. This is sometimes seen as a shortcoming in the city—and may well be one in fact— but it is certainly true to the spirit of Albuquerque.

For a third, it falls below the radar of an increasingly cynical media since it is not remarkable in any negative way. Its streets and freeways are busy but not congested. Its amazing skies are not extraordinarily polluted (October through February, the city does prohibit burning and discourages commuters from driving alone on days when the area's temperature inversion situation would keep the pollution from dispersing. In the last several years this has amounted to fewer than 20 days over the city's five months of winter).

This is compounded by the fact that Albuquerque is not prone to self-promotion. For all its immense but quiet pride in itself, the city still often seems forever trying to bolster its own low self-esteem. Although best-selling mystery novelist Tony Hillerman has called this home, none of the iconic figures who put New Mexico on the map in the early part of the century chose Albuquerque for his or her base of operations: D.H. Lawrence, Mabel Dodge Luhan, and Millicent Rogers all holed up in Taos; Mary Austin laid claim to Santa Fe; and Georgia O'Keeffe

retreated to the remote outpost of Abiquiu.

The city lacks the glamour of its siblings to the north, Santa Fe and Taos, and often suffers—even in its own eyes—in comparison. Santa Fe is entrancingly charming—richly historic, picturesque, replete with world-class shopping and dining, easygoing, and walkable. And Taos is gorgeous, old, tiny, indisputably if indescribably mystical. But both are primarily resort towns. Albuquerque is bigger, busier, more businesslike and industrial— a working city. Santa Fe was voted the best vacation destination in the world a few years ago by the discerning readers of *Condé Nast Traveler*, but in 1989, *Newsweek* magazine voted Albuquerque one of the ten best cities in America to live in. *Money* magazine voted it

the same in 1994, and a 1993 poll by the Ryder Consumer Truck Rental Division declared it the most popular relocation destination with a population of 100,000 or more in the United States.

Even in New Mexico, Albuquerque's days of playing third banana in the great triumvirate of northern cities may be passing, as these days it receives a fairly steady flow of relocators from both other cities.

For a city of its size, Albuquerque has shown remarkably little short-sightedness and a remarkable sense of itself and its place in the nation and the world. In the nearly 300 years since its official founding, the city may not always have shown a clear sense of where it was going, but neither can it be said ever to have lost its way. Now,

though, it is clearly headed forward. Unlike many ambitious cities that succeed as they progress, Albuquerque is not evolving by letting go of its history. It is a city with vision, looking squarely to the future, but one that knows equally well where it has been.

A LONG, RICH HISTORY

Albuquerque, which will officially turn 300 in the year 2006, is very old by American standards. Caves in the mountain range along its eastern edge offer evidence of habitation dating back thousands of years. Ruins along the banks of the Rio Grande, which bisects the city, are the remains of genuinely ancient civilizations. The venerable adobe pueblos that stud the interstate both north and south of town,

home to contemporary descen- dants of those civilizations, are hundreds of years older than the city. Evidence can place full-time occupation of the Rio Grande Valley about as early as A.D. 500. These valley dwellers were the early ancestors of the Pueblo Indians.

Among their most remarkable vestiges is Petroglyph National Monument on the west rim of the valley. It's estimated that possibly as early as 1000 B.C. they began pecking and scratching myriad drawings and pictographs into the rocks, resulting in one of the most impressive displays of prehistoric rock art in the Southwest. Exactly what they were conveying in these renderings of people, animals, and objects remains an archaeological mystery.

In the course of the following six centuries, this pre-Puebloan culture evolved considerably on its own and was additionally enriched by the arrival of peoples from other indigenous population cen- ters—particularly northern New Mexico, southwestern Colorado (Mesa Verde), and northeastern Arizona (Canyon de Chelly). This migration gave rise to, among many other things, sophisticated networks for transportation and communication throughout north- western New Mexico and the Four Corners area. By the end of the 14th century, experts estimate that at least 15,000 people were inhab- iting the middle Rio Grande Valley in permanent stone or adobe structures of several stories, and were cultivating crops including beans, squash, and corn—the

three mainstays of the healthy indigenous diet.

It was this group of settlements that the Spanish—a force of several hundred soldiers, slaves, and abundant livestock, under the command of the ambitious young Francisco Vásquez de Coronado—encountered when they ventured north from Compostela, Mexico, in 1540 on an expedition to claim for the king of Spain the treasures and riches of the mythical Seven Cities of Cibola.

Coronado's arrival was not the first appearance by the Spanish. Slave traders from Mexico had earlier made periodic forays into the area, capturing Indians to sell south of the border. But Coronado's grand entrance marked the arrival of the Spanish in earnest—a major turning point in the history of the state, and of at least three nations.

After an arduous journey north through Arizona and New Mexico, Coronado reached roughly what is now Rio Rancho and appears to have camped his force on the bank of the Rio Grande, near several constructed (and inhabited) pueblos. He chose to quarter his company in a pueblo through the winter (the remains of this pueblo now form the heart of Coronado State Monument just west of the city of Bernalillo). Coronado's conquistadors spent the winter of 1540-41 there, and stayed on as weather improved to use it as a headquarters from which to launch exploratory forays in search of the cities of gold. Although the Indians were at first generally amenable to the occupation, the Spanish quickly made themselves unwelcome, sparking a rebellion that ended disastrously for the Indians.

The treasure-seeking expedition was a virtually unabated disaster, and in difficulty and frustration Coronado found himself repeatedly violating his instructions to deal humanely and kindly with whatever peoples he might find. The first of those encounters had set the tone for the entire expedition. The first settlement they came to—which they anticipated as the first of the seven cities of Cibola—was actually one of the six pueblos or towns of the Zuni Indians. When its inhabitants failed to welcome the Spaniards, it was conquered with a violence sufficient to subdue the remaining Zuni pueblos. Over the course of the next two years, many Indians were killed, other pueblos were destroyed, food stores were plundered, and the search for treasure ended more or less as it had begun, with Coronado following yet another in a long succession of silver-tongued guides into the middle of nowhere. Coronado demanded an explanation and the guide confessed he intended to lead them to a remote spot and abandon them to their deaths. Coronado ordered the guide strangled to death.

Upon his empty-handed return, Coronado was tried for his cruelties to the native peoples. Although he was acquitted, his career as governor of one of the Spanish provinces of Mexico, and as a politician of great promise, was over.

He had found no gold or treasure, but he had blazed a trail and proven the possibility of exploring and perhaps colonizing the Southwest, launching a multitude of subsequent expeditions into the territory. Less than 60 years after Coronado returned to Mexico in disgrace, Don Juan de Oñate traveled into the new territory (by a more direct path than Coronado had taken) and laid claim to the entire region as the newest colony of the king of Spain. Oñate also named his route, which was followed by virtually all of the

explorers who succeeded Coronado, "El Camino Real." (Coronado's route had wandered first through Arizona; the Camino Real proceeded more directly from Mexico City clear to Taos. In its heyday, the Camino Real was an incomparable thoroughfare of commerce and communication.) Twelve years later, in 1610, the

> *He had found no gold or treasure, but he had blazed a trail and proven the possibility of exploring and perhaps colonizing the Southwest.*

Spanish established Santa Fe as the new colony's capital.

For several decades the colony was run efficiently, albeit not without friction between representatives of the Catholic church and the local bureaucrats and politi-

cians of the Spanish government— or between the church and the Indians it sought to Christianize at almost any cost. Finally, in 1680, the Indians exacted a measure of revenge for Coronado's depredations by rising up against their oppressors and killing a score of clerics and some 400 Spanish settlers. This was the Pueblo Revolt, and it united New Mexico's pueblos as nothing had before. Once the rebels had burned farmsteads, ranches and villages, and slaughtered men, women, and children in the outlying areas, they converged upon Santa Fe. Residents of the capital holed up with their livestock in the Palace of Governors for eleven days, until the Indians shut off their water supply by damming the creek that ran through the compound. When the governor and the townspeople emerged, the Indians allowed them to depart, and they fled south to El Paso. The Indians rebuffed Spanish attempts to reconquer the territory for the next twelve years, but in 1692

THE MERCANTILE PAST OF OLD TOWN IS ALIVE AND WELL IN THE ARRAY OF RESTAURANTS, ART AND CRAFT GALLERIES, AND CURIO SHOPS, AS WELL AS THE ASSEMBLY OF VENDORS (LEFT) WHO SET UP ON BLANKETS ON THE SIDEWALKS TO SELL AUTHENTIC HANDMADE JEWELRY TO PASSERSBY.
THE CITY COMES TOGETHER AT VARIOUS SPOTS FOR VARIOUS EVENTS. MARIACHI (RIGHT) IS ONLY ONE OF THE MANY KINDS OF MUSIC ON OFFER, REFLECTING THE CITY'S MULTICULTURAL HERITAGE.

Don Diego de Vargas marched north and took control without incident.

Subsequently, in the relative quiet of the Rio Grande Valley, where Albuquerque now lies, the Spanish established churches, villages, and vineyards. It was here that, among other things, the Catholic vintners found the most conducive climate in the New World for growing grapes to supply the colony's churches with sacristy wine. These early vineyards established the Albuquerque area as one of the oldest commercial wine-producing regions in all of North America. Although the area fell into disuse as a producer of wine grapes, it has now rebounded to the point that two French vintners have established the world headquarters of their wineries here, and have astonished the wine community with the quality of their vintages.

As the 18th century dawned in the valley, Spanish settlers occupied nearby areas in a series of large ranches and farms. One official community, Atrisco, had already been founded in the area, and the idea of founding an actual township in the river bosque was receiving much discussion.

In 1706, Don Francisco Cuervo y Valdez, the provisional governor of the colonial territory of New Mexico, petitioned to establish a villa here. Cuervo was a career government man, a characteristically ambitious bureaucrat in the Spanish hierarchy. His reasons for wanting to establish the villa were patriotic in that there was a genuine need for a Camino Real way station in the area, and self-serving

to the extent that he was eager to demonstrate to his superiors that he could bring order to the independent-minded territory.

But the Spanish had strict rules governing the establishment of villas in the territories. They had stipulated, for one thing, that a minimum of 30 families were required. By even his most opti-

> *In the relative quiet of the Rio Grande Valley, where Albuquerque now lies, the Spanish established churches, villages, and vineyards.*

mistic survey, Cuervo had no more than 18. It was a problem, but not a big one. Cuervo solved it by fibbing. However, believing that claiming a nice round 30 would look a little too convenient, he claimed the presence of 35 families. He built in a bit of insurance for himself by proposing to name the new settlement San Francisco Xavier de Alburquerque—in honor of Viceroy Francisco Fernández de la Cueva, the Duke of Alburquerque, who was responsible for preliminary approval of Cuervo's application. (This is the genesis of Albuquerque's nickname of "The Duke City.") Either the Viceroy saw Cuervo's maneuver for what it was and approved wholeheartedly, or Cuervo had learned his trick from his boss. In any event, the Viceroy did Cuervo one better, and changed the name

to San Felipe de Alburquerque to curry favor with his superior, the king of Spain (Saint Philip was the king's patron saint). The application was granted, and "Alburquerque" (the first "r" was later mysteriously dropped) was established, although Cuervo was subsequently tried in Mexico City on a series of charges—one of which being that he had lied to fulfill the requirements of the city's founding.

Mexico won its independence from Spain in 1821 and promptly opened New Mexico to trade with Americans. Only 25 years later, during the Mexican-American War, U.S. General Stephen Kearny went one step further and declared New Mexico a United States Territory— and established the little farm town as an official military outpost. As had the Spanish 150 years earlier, he stationed troops in the city to assist in defending the settlement against Indian attacks.

Many people quickly moved into the community in some numbers, opening shops which sold supplies to the troops and area farmers and ranchers. In 1862,

La Posada de Albuquerque (left) was built in 1939 by New Mexico native Conrad Hilton. A gorgeous, lavish example of Southwestern sophistication, the hotel was where Hilton honeymooned when he married Zsa Zsa Gabor—and was also famous enough that young airman Jimmy Stewart was rumored to fly in just for the green chile cheeseburgers served in the coffee shop. The hotel's charming, two-story lobby has become one of the city's classiest venues for quiet drinks or casual dancing.

THE PARTIALLY EXCAVATED RUINS OF KUAUA PUEBLO (ABOVE LEFT) STAND
AT THE HISTORIC CORONADO STATE MONUMENT, ON THE WEST BANK OF
THE RIO GRANDE. FROM 1934-39 THE MUSEUM OF NEW MEXICO, THE
UNIVERSITY OF NEW MEXICO, AND THE SCHOOL OF AMERICAN RESEARCH
CONDUCTED ARCHAEOLOGICAL INVESTIGATIONS HERE, DISCOVERING A NEARLY
INTACT SET OF MULTI-COLORED MURALS PAINTED ON SUCCESSIVE LAYERS OF
FRESH PLASTER INSIDE A KIVA. THESE MURALS OF HUMAN AND ANIMAL
FORMS ARE CONSIDERED AMONG THE FINEST EXAMPLES OF PREHISTORIC
MURAL ART IN NORTH AMERICA. THE WALLS OF THE KIVA WERE TRANSPORTED
TO THE UNIVERSITY WHERE EACH LAYER OF PLASTER WAS CAREFULLY
REMOVED AND ATTACHED TO MASONITE. THE MURALS CAN NOW BE SEEN IN
THE MONUMENT'S MUSEUM BUILDING.

ONE PARK SQUARE, BUILT IN 1984, AND TWO PARK SQUARE, BUILT IN 1987,
FORM THE CORPORATE AND COMMERCIAL HEART OF UPTOWN (ABOVE), THE
LARGEST AND MOST SUCCESSFUL MULTIPLE-USE DEVELOPMENT IN THE
STATE OF NEW MEXICO—AND THE ECONOMIC CENTER OF THE CITY OF
ALBUQUERQUE. SINCE THE MID-1970S, THE AREA HAS ATTRACTED SOME
$500 MILLION IN BUSINESS FROM SOME OF THE BEST UPSCALE CORPORATIONS
IN THE WORLD. IN ADDITION TO OFFICE COMPLEXES HOUSING STOCKBROKERS,
INSURANCE CORPORATIONS, ACCOUNTING FIRMS, MAJOR BANK BRANCHES,
LAW FIRMS, AND MORE, UPTOWN INCLUDES TWO THRIVING REGIONAL
SHOPPING MALLS, HOTELS, SPECIALTY RETAIL OUTLETS, AND A RICHLY VARIED
SELECTION OF RESTAURANTS—ALL IN ALL, SOME 4,200,000 SQUARE FEET OF
PRIVATE-SECTOR BUSINESS.

with the Civil War in its second year and the Confederate Army sweeping into the Southwest, Albuquerque's cadre of troops burned all the military supplies in town and abandoned the city, fleeing north to Santa Fe. There, they were joined by volunteers from Colorado, and proceeded east to Glorieta Pass, where they resoundingly defeated Confederate troops. The Confederates retreated to Albuquerque, where they implanted their cannons in the plaza. The Unionists pursued them and, in the ensuing artillery battle, beat them again. The Confederate commander ordered his cannons buried in the plaza and his troops out of the city.

The cannons were exhumed 30 years later. Albuquerque gave four of them to the Colorado Historical Society as a gesture of appreciation for the state's assistance in the skirmishes. Two are in the possession of the Albuquerque Museum.

Following the Civil War, the area's population began to increase rapidly. Merchants, tradesmen, artisans, doctors, and lawyers moved into

> *Down in Albuquerque, however, a singular German immigrant, entrepreneur, merchant, and real-estate developer, Franz Huning, saw the railroad as the making of the town— and his fortune.*

the state and began establishing businesses. These entrepreneurs found it highly advantageous to conform to the dominant Hispanic society; many learned to speak Spanish, and married into Albuquerque's established families.

Within 15 years, by 1880, the railroad had crossed roughly half of New Mexico. It had planned to build a depot, offices, railroad yard, and roundhouse in Bernalillo, then head south in a straight line, thus strategically avoiding a big bend in the Rio Grande. Don José Leandro Perea, whose family owned most of the land in Bernalillo, offered to sell the railroad all the land it needed—for $425 an acre.

Down in Albuquerque, however, a singular German immigrant, entrepreneur, merchant, and real-estate developer, Franz Huning, saw the railroad as the making of the town—and his fortune. Huning operated a steam-powered flour mill southeast of the Plaza, had co-founded the Bridge Company (which built the first modern bridge across the Rio Grande), served as first president of the *Albuquerque Journal*, and much more. Huning organized a

IT WOULD BE VIRTUALLY IMPOSSIBLE TO OVERSTATE THE IMPORTANCE OF THE RAILROAD IN THE HISTORY OF THE CITY AND COUNTRY. LEGEND HAS IT THAT THE RAILROAD IS RESPONSIBLE FOR THE BASTARDIZATION OF THE CITY'S VERY NAME—CLAIMING THAT A RAILROAD SIGN-PAINTER EITHER FORGOT OR HAD NO ROOM FOR A SECOND "R" THAT DISAPPEARED MYSTERIOUSLY FROM THE CITY'S ORIGINAL NAME OF "ALBURQUERQUE." IT WAS THE RAILROAD THAT REVERSED THE ETHNIC BALANCE OF THE POPULATION, TRANSFORMING IT INTO A PREDOMINANTLY WHITE CITY IN ONLY FIVE YEARS. ANOTHER RESULT OF THE RAILROAD'S ARRIVAL WAS THE ALVARADO HOTEL (ABOVE, PHOTO COURTESY OF THE ALBUQUERQUE MUSEUM), THE GRANDLY-SCALED, SHOWPIECE OF THE HARVEY HOUSE RAILROAD-HOTEL CHAIN. OVER THE YEARS, THE HOTEL HOUSED AUGUST GUESTS INCLUDING JACK BENNY, JOAN CRAWFORD, ALBERT EINSTEIN, KATHERINE HEPBURN, CHARLES LINDBERGH, RUDOLPH VALENTINO, AND PRESIDENTS TAFT, HOOVER, WILSON, AND BOTH ROOSEVELTS. OPENED IN 1902, THE SPLENDID OLD HOTEL WAS DEMOLISHED IN 1970, BUT REMAINS FOR MANY THE TRUE SYMBOL OF THE CITY.

cadre of local businessmen, including William Hazeldine and Elias Stover, who began buying up the land where the tracks would lie. They then made the railroad an offer it simply couldn't refuse, selling it all the land it needed for a grand total of $1, including some surplus land along the right-of-way. This the railroad was free to sell to developers, although profits had to be split with Huning's company. Not surprisingly, the railroad accepted the terms.

The station was built one mile east of the plaza, essentially creating two separate Albuquerques—the long-extant one centered in the plaza, called Old Town, and a new one right around the depot—which was promptly named New Town. The old and the new were connected by Railroad Avenue (now Central). People shuttled back and forth between them aboard a mule-drawn streetcar—an operation of the Street Railway

Company, in which Huning was also involved.

The impact of the railroad's arrival is almost incalculable. Within five years, so many newcomers had arrived that they composed a majority of the city's population. Within the same period, the Albuquerque Gas Company was organized, the first telephone system was in place, the Albuquerque Water Company was formed, and incandescent lights began shining in the city's homes.

The railroad brought about another profoundly influential development. In 1853, under the auspices of Archbishop Lamy, the Loretto Sisters founded the Academy of Our Lady of Light, which later became known as Loretto Academy. In 1865, Lamy summoned the Sisters of Charity of Cincinnati, Ohio, to Santa Fe to establish the St. Vincent Orphanage and Hospital. Fifteen years later, when trains began rolling into Albuquerque, the Sisters opened Wayfarer's House in Old Town to care for the sick among the multitudes of newcomers. In 1902, they dedicated the St. Joseph Sanatorium, the forerunner of St. Joseph Hospital on Martin Luther King Avenue.

Albuquerque's mild year-round climate and high, dry air swiftly earned the city a worldwide reputation as an ideal place to recover from respiratory diseases. It drew huge numbers of sufferers seeking treatment, and their families (the patients were called, not especially solicitously, "lungers"). In response, individuals and agencies began building recuperation hospitals throughout the city. Lungers represented such an influx of new residents—many of whom would prove to be pillars of local society and have enormous influence on the city—that Albuquerque came to be called "The City That Bad Lungs Built."

In 1908, Presbyterian minister Hugh Albert Cooper oversaw the dedication of Presbyterian's sana-

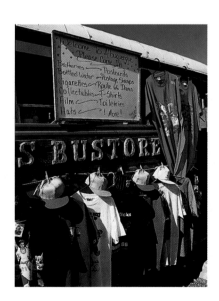

torium. In 1913, a promising young physician from Missouri, William R. Lovelace, moved to Albuquerque to cure his own tuberculosis. Lovelace was a man of vision, and he had taken note of what he considered the wave of the future in medicine: group medical practice. He made a series of trips east to the Mayo Clinic to study that operation, and in 1922 formed a partnership in Albuquerque with a friend and fellow physician and TB sufferer, Edgar T. Lassetter. Although the

> *Albuquerque's mild year-round climate and high, dry air swiftly earned the city a worldwide reputation as an ideal place to recover from respiratory diseases.*

idea of a group practice met with resistance initially, by 1940—with the city's population at 35,000—the practice was thriving.

Albuquerque became the official site of the University of New Mexico in 1889, following some wily negotiation with the state's other big cities and the decisive contribution of all the land needed to house the campus. The first building, Hodgin Hall, a tall brick structure housing the whole of the university, was completed in 1892. In 1901, William Tight became president of the university—an act which generated little remark at the time but which would prove

one of the most significant milestones in the city's history.

Tight felt that architecture should arise from the traditions of its context, and began working with architect E.B. Cristy to come up with an amalgam of indigenous regional elements—a brand-new style that came to be known as "Pueblo Revival." He began designing campus buildings that borrowed and incorporated elements from the structures on the many nearby pueblos, transforming the campus into what some have described as "a symbol of New Mexico regionalism."

In 1908, Tight replaced the gabled roof of Hodgin Hall with a flat one and stuccoed the exterior to resemble adobe. Although Tight is widely praised today, and although he was proud of having turned the school into a "pueblo on the mesa," in some senses he martyred himself to the cause of architectural regionalism; he was fired for his perceived desecration of Hodgin Hall. It didn't take the university long to see the error of its ways; in 1927 the school declared "pueblo style" its official architecture. One of the style's chief practitioners, the brilliant Santa Fe architect John Gaw Meem, made the campus into the world's

greatest Pueblo Revival showcase and made a name for himself in the history of architecture.

Perhaps most ironically, Pueblo Revival remains one of the most enduring holdovers from the period, a predominant influence still abundantly evident. The style is manifested in the jutting vigas, adobe-colored stucco, crenelated

roofs, kiva fireplaces, beamed ceilings, and tile floors that characterize many of even the least aesthetically concerned housing developments.

Albuquerque had remained largely untouched by the First World War, but it played a much more significant role in World War II. In 1940, the military had established a service station for its aircraft at Albuquerque Army Air Base, south of town. In 1941, with American involvement imminent in the expanding war, the military established the Air Corps Advanced Flying School there. In 1943, the Army laid claim to an affluent boys' school on a mesa high above Santa Fe and established the Manhattan Project there to build the world's first atomic bomb. The base was renamed Kirtland Field and from 1942 to 1945 the little Albuquerque facility, which later became Kirtland Air Force Base, was integrally involved in the project.

After the war Kirtland was estabished as the site of Sandia

National Laboratories, a highly restricted munitions, research and development facility. Sandia's importance increased in the Cold War, when the base became a center for some of the most sophisticated and highest-level scientific and technological exploration in the world. So Kirtland kept growing, and Sandia, even while maintaining a very low public profile, has helped Albuquerque earn a reputation as one of the world's top high-tech research and development sites.

The city's burgeoning technological reputation got another boost in 1947, when William Lovelace's nephew, Randy, returned to Albuquerque and joined his uncle's practice. A flight surgeon and an expert in aviation medicine, Randy was a colonel in the U.S. Army Air Forces, the predecessor of the Air Force, during World War II. He was also a member of the three-man team that developed the first oxygen mask. Randy had further distinguished himself by volunteering to test the mask—using it in a jump from a plane at 40,200 feet. In addition to helping put his uncle's group practice on the secure footing that enabled it to expand with such phenomenal success, in 1959 Randy put his aviation medicine experience to further use by devising for NASA an extensive series of tests to judge the fitness of candidates for travel in outer space. These were the tests administered as part of the selection process in choosing America's Mercury astronauts— the process documented in Tom Wolfe's *The Right Stuff*.

A VIBRANT PRESENT, A PROMISING FUTURE

Today, Albuquerque and Bernalillo County are a striking celebration of contrasts. The first indication of this is the way this area surprises the traveler. In a sparsely populated, barely even ruralized desert landscape, it opens like a vast, sprawling oasis of civilization, rich with lawns and flowers and fountains and water. With fourteen centuries of history and prehistoric caves in its mountains, the area is also a center of some of the most advanced scientific and technological research and development in the world—a place where any number of the weapons and technological innovations of the future are taking shape.

For many people, it retains its

decades-outmoded reputation as a sleepy little rest stop on Route 66, where residents live mostly to pump gas, repair flats and blown or overheated engines, serve green-chile cheeseburgers, and supply rooms for parched and weary families driving from Chicago to Los Angeles.

But Albuquerque and Bernalillo County are a highly successful, hard-working duo, boasting a university with a medical school consistently ranked in the top ten in the nation, being the state seat of federal government, and housing the biggest and most productive manufacturing facility of the largest single producer of computer chips in the world.

The local Indian pueblos, under careful and sometimes canny man-

agement, are making the most of the often meager resources they've been allotted. Many pueblos have also sought economic advancement by employing their lands as resorts, fishing and sporting venues, and development communities. The pueblo gambling casinos, though controversial, bring in revenue used for a variety of social services. The All Indian Pueblo Council, a consortium comprised of 19 pueblo governments, oversaw the creation of the Indian Pueblo Cultural Center, completed in 1976. The center houses two museums, shops, a book room, an archive, and a restaurant serving native food. The center showcases cultural artifacts and information about the pueblos and sponsors traditional native dances on the weekends

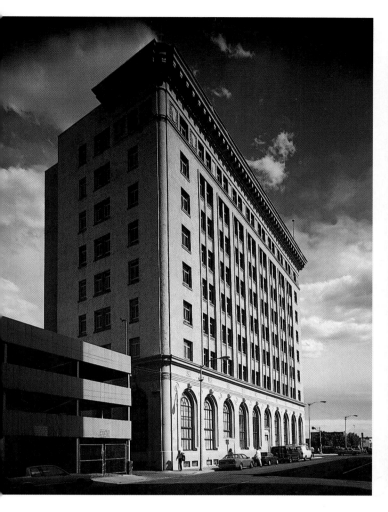

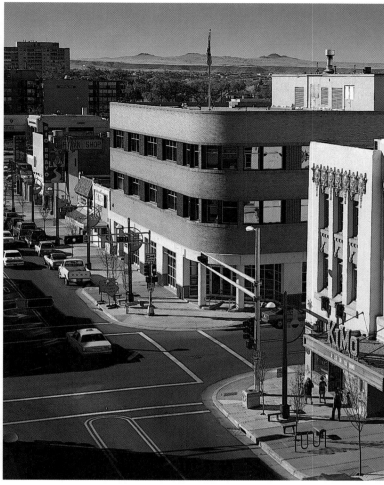

ALBUQUERQUE IS A CITY WITH A LONG HISTORY OF ARRESTING ARCHITECTURE, AND WITH PLENTY OF IT ON UNOSTENTATIOUS DISPLAY, FROM THE ARCHED COLONNADE OF THE LAWYERS TITLE BUILDING (ABOVE FAR LEFT) AND THE GLASS WALL OF 320 GOLD (ABOVE LEFT)—REFLECTING THE HYATT HOTEL AND THE BANK OF AMERICA BUILDING—TO THE VERTICALITY OF THE FIRST NATIONAL BANK BUILDING (ABOVE). THERE IS ALSO THE INTERSECTION OF CONTRAST DOWNTOWN WHERE THE HISTORIC "PUEBLO DECO" KIMO THEATER (NAMED IN A CONTEST BY THE GOVERNOR OF NEARBY ISLETA PUEBLO, IN WHOSE TEWA LANGUAGE "KIMO" WAS THE NAME FOR "MOUNTAIN LION") FACES UPSCALE STREAMLINE MODERNE (ABOVE RIGHT), BOTH OF THEM BACKDROPPED BY THE FIVE CONES OF DORMANT VOLCANOES ON THE CITY'S WEST SIDE.

and special events year round.

They have also succeeded in retaining significant portions of their traditional lifeways. Virtually all of the pueblos are open to considerate sightseers and still hold feast days, festivities, and celebrations, many of which respectful visitors are welcome to attend. In addition to the pueblo presence, there are Navajos residing in western Bernalillo County and thousands of members of numerous other tribes living in the city.

The city and county have become leading vacation destinations. Possessing one of the highest per-capita concentrations of restaurants in the country, the city is deservedly praised for its superb food, regional and otherwise. It is a shopping mecca for customers

from Arizona, Utah, Colorado, Oklahoma, and Texas as well as throughout New Mexico. It is home to one of the five biggest and most successful state fairs in the nation. And it invented and annually hosts the biggest public hot air ballooning event in the world.

It is not too grand to say that few metro areas in the world can boast to the abundance of diversity that this one can. Use the word "diversity" today and you open yourself to charges of political correctness. But here the word means not simply ethnic or "cultural" diversity, but diversity in everything— people, lifestyles, landscapes, environment, architecture, natural and recreational resources, and economy. It is, for example,

one of the few places on earth where you can ski in the morning and golf in the afternoon—and spend less than half an hour driving from one to the other.

After World War II, the city might well have expected a build-down in the facilities at Kirtland Air Force Base. Instead, the base began expanding rapidly, and the expansion led to accelerated residential development directly north of the base to house the influx of new military and civilian personnel. The new housing gave rise to commercial development, as merchants and others set up to serve this exploding new market. San Mateo, San Pedro, Louisiana boulevards—at one time these were the easternmost reaches of the city. Now, however, they form the spine of its fastest growing sec-

tion. The newer stores and markets that sprang up in the area began drawing shoppers and customers away from the city's Downtown. In the early 1950s, two developers capitalized on this rapidly expanding market by building shopping malls practically across the street from one another, right in the middle of this burgeoning area. Less than a decade later, President Eisenhower established the federal interstate highway system. In Albuquerque the east-west interstate ran within a half-mile of both malls, making them accessible and convenient from virtually anywhere in the city. The shift away from Downtown was complete, and the traditional heart of the city slipped into a long period of benign neglect. When, in 1988, a Dallas architecture critic took

stock of the city, his appraisal was bleak: "One large pocket of despair is Downtown, one of the hardest and most hostile in the country."

A number of steps have been taken over the last decade to revitalize the area. Some have met with resistance or indifference—a proposed performing arts center on the Civic Plaza was defeated by voters, and a disused 1929 wool and fur warehouse in the area was splendidly transformed in 1985 into a dinner theater but soon failed, and has met with no greater success in any of several incarnations since.

But several of the city's efforts have been both ambitious and successful, and Downtown continues to enjoy considerable support from proponents who feel that a great downtown is a crucial com-

ponent of any truly great city. In 1989, the city council approved a comprehensive formal Downtown Core Revitalization Strategy. One year later, construction was completed on an expansion (begun in 1985) of the city's Downtown convention center. The project, which enlarged the center by 106,000 square feet and enhanced it aesthetically by an exponential factor, transformed the facility into one that could attract and accommodate large groups and major events. It was a success by any measure, and in 1994 the center and the Albuquerque Convention and Visitors Bureau hosted its largest gathering in the city's history, the massive annual convention of the International Association of Chiefs of Police, parts of which were televised nationally and at which President Clinton was a surprise guest speaker. Albuquerque's master plan calls for more enhancements Downtown: more exhibit space in the convention center and construction of two more major hotels in the area.

In 1990, Albuquerque Plaza office and commercial tower and the Hyatt Hotel both opened Downtown, giving the city its two tallest buildings. In 1994, the city, faced with the necessity of replacing 60-year-old water lines and silty soil beneath Central Avenue, saw an opportunity in the looming demolition and reconstruction. A local architectural firm devised a construction plan that combined the necessary project with the broader municipal goal of revitalizing the area. The plan took steps to help clear the traffic con-

gestion along the street. It also widened the sidewalks, installed brighter streetlights to increase the area's use after dark, and provided new landscaping (including some 130 young trees), bike racks, and a clock tower.

The city has now seized a similar opportunity to perform a multimillion dollar renovation of the 200,000-square-foot civic plaza. The presence of a sprawling sculptural fountain (which has come to symbolize Downtown Albuquerque for many of the city's residents) and a series of large flower-filled planter boxes notwithstanding, the plaza conveys a predominant impression of being little more than a large expanse of concrete. A local architectural firm has been contracted to capitalize on the need to replace the waterproofing membrane beneath the surface of the plaza by transforming the plaza itself. The project will add turf areas, an elevated stage capable of accommodating a full symphony orchestra, a cable-supported fabric shade structure, and large metal trellises that will double as shelters for food vendors at the city's popular multiethnic Summerfest

events. Of the original appurtenances, only the fountain will remain.

And even in the crucial matter of whether Downtown is capable of surviving on its own in a free-market sense, the area is on the upswing. It continues to evolve as the city's densest concentration of nightlife venues and options, with galleries, live music in clubs and bars, a resurgent if still struggling theater scene, a brewpub, a handful of the city's finest restaurants,

(PREVIOUS PAGES) THE FOURTH STREET PEDESTRIAN MALL, WHICH RUNS FOR TWO BLOCKS FROM GRAND TO CENTRAL DOWNTOWN, IS AN OASIS OF GREENERY AND SHADE IN THE MIDST OF HIGH-RISES AND PARKING GARAGES—A SUMMER HAVEN FOR DOWNTOWNERS ON LUNCH BREAK. LIKE ANY BUSTLING BUSINESS DISTRICT, DOWNTOWN ALBUQUERQUE IS ALIVE WITH PEOPLE (AND PEOPLE-WATCHERS), FROM NEW MEXICO ARTIST GLENNA GOODACRE'S REALISTIC SCULPTURE *SIDEWALK SOCIETY* (LEFT) TO THE THOUSANDS OF REAL-LIFE PROFESSIONALS, EXECUTIVES, AND OFFICE WORKERS WHO COMMUTE INTO THE AREA IN CARS, ON BUSES, BIKES, AND FOOT (ABOVE). GOODACRE'S WORK STANDS AT THE SOUTHWEST CORNER OF 3RD AND TIJERAS. HER OTHER WORKS INCLUDE THE WOMEN'S VIETNAM MEMORIAL IN WASHINGTON, D.C.

and a growing number of new ones.

Albuquerque is perhaps best perceived as a collection of these types of communities—each serving as a separate "city center." The great appeal of these centers is that they form more immediately accessible smaller neighborhoods, each offering a distinct and more or less clearly defined lifestyle choice. In Albuquerque, these centers complement rather than compete against one another, deeply enriching the life of the city. They are, in fact, the very elements of the area that gave the city its diverse charm and variegated personality in the first place—and continue to do so. They are what

give the big city of Albuquerque its sense of accessibility and comprehensibility, its profoundly appealing sense of innocence, and its astonishing ability not to overwhelm.

Downtown is one of these centers, of course. It is a unique central place built around the center of government, and it can be argued that it is the city's only truly urban center (other commercial areas feeling distinctly more suburban). Other "centers" throughout the city include the South Valley, the airport, the university area, the Northeast Heights, the West Mesa, North Albuquerque, and the environs of the Albuquerque Academy.

The intrinsic diversity of these constituent neighborhoods is one of the city's great strengths and true distinctions, and Albuquerque has taken a major step to preserve them as such. In June of 1995, the city council formally approved the Community Identity Program. With that approval the city boldly accomplished two important

ends—it embraced its historic pattern of development, and it reinforced the value of existing communities and neighborhoods.

In a city growing as fast as Albuquerque is, there is the danger that the city grows so quickly that the centers will be subsumed into a larger whole that is less differentiated, more homogenized, and consequently less interesting and appealing. Formally establishing Albuquerque as a city of neighborhoods is also a way of preserving the city's uniqueness, of celebrating the cultural richness of its exceptionally diverse components. The business community, too, has begun to see that there is a direct relationship between the quality of Albuquerque and the business climate.

Over a period of two years, the city held nine public workshops at various locations, canvassing residents of Albuquerque's different areas to determine where those residents shop, work, play, go to school, and so on. Armed with that information, planners broke the city down into ten "community planning areas"—West Side, North Valley, North Albuquerque, Central Albuquerque, Near Heights, Mid-Heights, Foothills, Southwest Mesa, South Valley, and East Gateway. Each of these areas contains a central or major regional center and several smaller community centers.

The program has ramifications through all aspects of community planning. It will dramatically localize civic spending, regulations, service needs, and more, and will cross all traditional boundaries within city govern-

BERNALILLO COUNTY IS UNIQUE IN MANY
WAYS, ONE OF WHICH IS THAT IT'S A
METROPOLITAN AREA OF HALF A MILLION
PEOPLE (ONE THIRD OF THE POPULATION
OF THE ENTIRE STATE) WHICH STILL
CONTAINS ABUNDANT EVIDENCE OF A
DEEP-ROOTED RURAL CHARACTER,
PARTICULARLY AT BOTH ENDS OF THE
RIVER VALLEY—A CHARACTER EVIDENT IN
THIS SOUTH VALLEY CORNFIELD (ABOVE
RIGHT) STRETCHING FROM SECOND
STREET TO THE DENSE CORRIDOR OF
TREES ON THE BANKS OF THE RIO GRANDE.
THE RURAL TRADITIONS LIVE ON IN SOME
UNEXPECTED LOCATIONS, LIKE THE HI-LO
MARKET, WHERE PRODUCE MANAGER
CHARLES PERKINS CUSTOM ROASTS FRESH
GREEN CHILES FOR CUSTOMERS (BELOW).
BUT THE COUNTY BRIDGES THE GAP
BETWEEN PAST AND PRESENT WITH AN
INDUSTRIAL BASE ENCOMPASSING EVERY-
THING FROM THREE-PIECE PROFESSIONAL-
ISM TO FACTORY LABOR (BELOW RIGHT).

Albuquerque's reputation as a center of cutting-edge technological experimentation and innovation has been known to insiders for some 50 years, primarily owing to the fact that most of the work was related to defense and the military. The city was instrumental in the development of the atomic bomb, and a full-size replica of Fat Man (below left), the bomb dropped on Hiroshima, resides in the National Atomic Museum on Kirtland Air Force Base in the city.

Now, the city is so well known as a center of high-tech that the area has been dubbed "the Silicon Mesa," and Sandia Laboratories (below far left - Official U.S. Air Force Photo by Arthur J. Goodman) is largely responsible for this moniker.

Intel (above) has also positioned itself at the high-tech forefront. With its first local fabrication plant, built in 1980, Intel essentially put the exploding Albuquerque suburb of Rio Rancho on the map. Following more than a decade of steady growth at the site, the company rewarded the city by deciding to locate a five-year, $2 billion expansion project here. Bill Sheppard (above left, pictured with a Pentium 90 chip) is site manager of the Rio Rancho plant.

ment. It is explicitly designed to increase civic pride and community identity, and to empower the individual neighborhoods to become pro-active —collaborating with city government rather than depending upon it.

In 1994, a new home was built for the South Broadway Cultural Center, combining a branch library, performing and visual arts venues, and meeting and multi-purpose facilities. The new center is far more beautiful and almost five times larger than the old. Subsidized with a $2.5 million bond issue, it created a major cultural attraction in a neighborhood many city residents have never even entered—a clear demonstration of the city's commitment to the area.

Nob Hill, an area that felt the impact, along with Downtown, of the malls and the interstates, has rebounded in part due to an active merchants' association. The association printed maps of the district, and installed signs on area streetlight standards designating it the

Nob Hill Historic District. In 1994, the city's Public Art Program funded construction of neon-accented arches across Central Avenue demarcating the more or less official ends of the district. Nob Hill today is arguably the city's most sophisticated stretch of antique stores, outstanding restaurants, high-end clothing boutiques, and hip general merchandise shops.

But it's not only the business districts that have begun moving toward greater localization. Albuquerque is home to more than 220 separate grassroots neighborhood associations, all established by the residents of each neighborhood, all bespeaking a mixture of pride and concern, self-interest and community spirit. The neighborhood association movement has taken such hold in Albuquerque that the city operates an Office of Neighborhood Coordination to serve as a liaison between the associations and local government, holding workshops, publishing an association directory

and a monthly newsletter.

The city has been wise in devising mechanisms to generate the funds needed for its improvements and special projects. Revenues from the Lodger's Tax, levied on the city's hotel beds, will fund the renovation of the Civic Plaza. But the most progressive accomplishments have been funded through an innovative Quality of Life Tax, enacted by the city council in 1988 and responsible for generating some $150 million. These funds have paid in part or in whole for purchases of considerable open space, including acreage in the Sandia foothills and parcels now contained in Petroglyph National Monument—purchases that preserved both areas from further development. Tax revenues have also gone toward purchase of land for and construction of a long planned Balloon Museum. This estimated $23 million project will combine the world's most comprehensive museum on hot air ballooning, a permanent home for

(PREVIOUS PAGES) IN APRIL ALBUQUERQUE HOSTS THE GATHERING OF NATIONS POWWOW—THE BIGGEST POWWOW IN NORTH AMERICA. THIS IS A MASSIVE SPECTACLE WITH COSTUMED DANCERS AND OTHER NATIVE PERFORMERS, AND OFFERINGS FROM ALL ASPECTS OF NATIVE AMERICAN CULTURE.

ALBUQUERQUE'S GROWING SCHEDULE OF CONVENTIONS LED TO THE EXPANSION OF ITS DOWNTOWN CONVENTION CENTER (ABOVE FAR LEFT) IN 1990—TURNING IT INTO A STATE-OF-THE-ART FACILITY.

IN 1995, ALBUQUERQUE PLAYED HOST TO THE PRESTIGIOUS JAPAN-AMERICA WEEK, AND THE CITY'S BROAD-RANGING MULTI-CULTURALISM WAS INTERWOVEN WITH YET ANOTHER THREAD. AMONG THE HIGH-LIGHTS WAS A PERFORMANCE BY JAPANESE TAIKO DRUMMERS AT THE CITY'S INDIAN PUEBLO CULTURAL CENTER (ABOVE LEFT).

IN WHAT AMOUNTS TO A LIVING MUSEUM EXHIBIT, THE CITY'S FOUNDER'S DAY CELEBRATIONS INCLUDE A BRILLIANTLY COLORFUL PARADE (ABOVE).

ALL THAT GLITTERS IS NOT IN CONVEN-TION EXHIBIT HALLS, HOWEVER. PREEMINENT ALBUQUERQUE RESTAURATEUR DAVE GARDUÑO HAS A PORTION OF HIS EXCEPTIONAL AUTOMOBILE COLLECTION ON DISPLAY IN THE YESTERDAVE'S AUTO MUSEUM (ABOVE RIGHT).

the world-renowned Kodak© Albuquerque International Balloon Fiesta, and a year-round park with sports fields, general use facilities and picnic areas. With the help of a grant from the United States Air Force, Quality of Life funds are also responsible for a new chil-dren/science center, a collaborative effort of the University of New Mexico's Department of Astronomy, the Albuquerque Children's Museum, and Explora!. The Biological Park on the bank of the Rio Grande is the most ambi-tious Quality of Life project. The park comprises a first-class aquari-um and botanical gardens. This project also entails dramatic improvements to the city's rather neglected Tingley Beach recreation area, which will receive two new lakes—one for fishing, one for model boating—and general enhancements to improve its atmosphere for families and pic-nickers. The Quality of Life funds have also been applied to meet less luxurious needs: they've helped

pay for improvements to streets and storm drains, and the addition of 50 officers to the city's police force.

Having implemented the Community Identity and Quality of Life programs, the city is uniquely well prepared and strate-gically positioned to move into the 21st century.

The city's 19th-century boom-market, the sanatorium industry, has resumed its position of importance in the region. Considerably broader in mission now than it was 120 years ago, the hospitals are now huge, thriving corporations, and have trans-formed Albuquerque into a leader and a national model in health care. In 1992, Russel J. Coile, presi-dent of Health Forecasting Group, declared Albuquerque one of the top five health care cities in the nation—a city whose health care agencies were forging partnerships that could well serve as models for the rest of the country. That same year, a report to the National

Committee for Quality Health Care declared Albuquerque "an ideal place to take a first, close look at the future of health care delivery."

William Lovelace's eponymous two-man practice is today one of the biggest health care providers in the nation—with dedicated divisions making it a national leader in medical research and education. Presbyterian Hospital, which admitted 30 patients with tuberculosis when it opened in 1908, is now the largest hospital system in the state, with a network of three hospitals and four urgent-care treatment centers in the Albuquerque area alone, a roster of some 23,000 medical admissions

each year, and a record of delivering nearly half of all babies born in Bernalillo County.

The University of New Mexico's Cancer Center is widely regarded as a facility producing leading cancer research and offering highly innovative, cutting-edge treatment protocols, as well as more traditional treatment. *U.S. News & World Report* has for several years rated the university's School of Medicine one of the top ten medical schools in the United States for primary care. It has served as a model for, among others, Harvard School of Medicine, which sent a delegation out to study the school's primary-care curriculum.

But probably the most promising industry, high technology—long a low-profile, secret industry in Albuquerque—has come above ground with something of a vengeance. The city's high-tech profile has risen to the point that the metro area has been dubbed "the Silicon Mesa" in the national media.

Kirtland Air Force Base and Sandia Labs remain exceptionally healthy engines driving a thriving local high-technology industry, even if much of their work remains hidden from public eyes. The base and the labs are still largely working in the hush-hush world of nuclear and weapons research, but the labs are also making strides and contributions in defense conversion and many other fields, such as high speed trains and structural analysis.

In the private sector, Intel Corporation, the world's largest single manufacturer of computer chips, almost single-handedly gave the city an industrial economic base when it first arrived in the area in 1980 and built a fabrication facility in Rio Rancho. Multiple expansions in the interim culminated in the 1993 launch of a five-year, $2 billion project adding 1.8 million square feet to the facility and several thousand new jobs to the company's payroll. While the site had long been significant, that addition tipped the balance for several of Intel's suppliers, who quickly announced intentions to move into the area, either relocating or building new facilities here.

But the specifics may not, in the end, matter that much. One of the lessons that seems clear from Albuquerque and Bernalillo County's history is that their durability, resiliency, and instincts have seen them through periods of challenge and difficulty that would have taken permanent tolls on less flexible cities. Watching the area deal with challenges, in fact, is one of the great satisfac-

> *Albuquerque and Bernalillo County are a sumptuous feast of surprises, of options and alternatives, of diversity, of contrasts and complements.*

tions of living here. In spite of their age, Albuquerque and Bernalillo County feel both contemporary and exceptionally open-minded. They continue to change constantly—and to welcome that change.

Albuquerque and Bernalillo County are a sumptuous feast of surprises, of options and alternatives, of diversity, of contrasts and complements. They are rich, flexible, accommodating, and appealing to an enormous range of tastes. They are a feast, but not—alas, and thank God—a moveable one. To partake fully of this region, you must be here, where it is happening, where it is changing, where it is getting better and better with every passing day.

(PREVIOUS PAGES) THE NEW MEXICO STATE FAIR IS THE SECOND LARGEST STATE FAIR IN NORTH AMERICA. RIDES (ABOVE LEFT) AND GAMES OF CHANCE FILL THE MIDWAY; FARMERS AND FUTURE FARMERS SHOW OFF THE TALENTS OF THEIR LIVESTOCK IN VARIOUS BARNS (LEFT); AND MAKERS OF EVERYTHING FROM TWISTY FRIES TO BARBECUED TURKEY LEGS MAKE SURE THAT THE MORE THAN ONE MILLION PEOPLE IN ATTENDANCE CAN GET PLENTY OF FOOD FAST. THE FAIRGROUNDS ARE HOME TO AN ASTOUNDING VARIETY OF SPECIAL AND ANNUAL EVENTS BESIDES THE FAIR. THESE INCLUDE RODEOS, ARTS AND CRAFTS FAIRS, SEASONAL HORSE RACING AT THE ON-PREMISES ALBUQUERQUE DOWNS, AND A MAMMOTH WEEKLY FLEA MARKET.
(FOLLOWING PAGES) DATING BACK TO 1927 AND STILL OPERATING AS A MULTI-USE THEATER AND PERFORMANCE VENUE, THE LANDMARK KiMo THEATER REPRESENTS A GREAT EXAMPLE OF THE BOLD "PUEBLO DECO" STYLE.
(PAGES 62-63) AT SECOND AND GOLD STREETS DOWNTOWN, ONE OF THE CITY'S MANY SPECTACULAR MURALS DEPICTS THE HEYDAY OF THE RAILROAD, WITH A SWEEPING LOCOMOTIVE DRAWING UP BEFORE THE WORLD-FAMOUS ALVARADO HOTEL.

BEAUTIFULLY LANDSCAPED, CENTRALLY LOCATED, AND EASILY ACCESSIBLE, UPTOWN IN THE 1960S VIRTUALLY REPLACED DOWNTOWN AS THE CITY'S FOREMOST CONCENTRATION OF COMMERCIAL ENTERPRISES. TODAY, THE AREA BOASTS MORE THAN ONE AND ONE HALF MILLION SQUARE FEET OF MULTIUSE COMMERCIAL SPACE IN A SETTING INCLUDING SEA PLAZA (LEFT, BUILT IN 1985, 94,243 SQUARE FEET), THE CITADEL (ABOVE, BUILT IN 1984, 100,000 SQUARE FEET), AND CITY CENTRE (BELOW, BUILT IN 1974, 174,339 SQUARE FEET).

ALBUQUERQUE MAKES NO SECRET OF ITS APPRECIATION FOR SERIOUS ART, AND HAS A HIGHLY SUCCESSFUL PROGRAM FOSTERING THE COMMISSION AND PLACEMENT OF PUBLIC ART THROUGHOUT THE CITY. BUT IT'S A CITY WITH ROOM, TOO, FOR MORE PLAYFUL *OBJETS*. THE CRIMSON STEEL ARROW AT CARLISLE AND INDIAN SCHOOL (LEFT) MARKS INDIAN PLAZA SHOPPING CENTER. THE CONCRETE PLASTER COWBOY (ABOVE) HAS STARED LEVELLY OUT ACROSS INTERSTATE 25 FROM THE PARKING LOT OF THE CARPET COMPANY FOR SOME 20 YEARS. AND A ROUGH-HEWN PAUL BUNYAN (BELOW RIGHT) OF UNCERTAIN PROVENANCE STANDS ABOVE A KENTUCKY FRIED CHICKEN OUTLET AT THE CORNER OF A GAS STATION PARKING LOT ON CENTRAL. A PRODUCT OF THE CITY'S PUBLIC ART PROGRAM, *CRUISING SAN MATEO I* (ABOVE RIGHT), ON SAN MATEO AT GIBSON, HAS BEEN WIDELY, BLITHELY DERIDED WITH THE NICKNAME "CHEVY ON A STICK," BUT IT COMBINES WITH *CRUISING SAN MATEO II* AND *CRUISING SAN MATEO III* TO PRESENT ARTIST BARBARA GRYGUTIS' PORTRAIT OF SAN MATEO BOULEVARD AS THE ECONOMIC BACKBONE OF THE CITY DURING THE 1950S, THE MOST DRAMATIC DECADE OF GROWTH FOR ALBUQUERQUE.

(FOLLOWING PAGES) THE *RISTRA*, THE BUNCH OF CHILES HANGING TO DRY IN THE SUN, BEGAN AS A UTILITARIAN TRADITION BUT HAS BECOME AN ELEMENT OF SOUTHWESTERN DESIGN AS PREVALENT AS THE MOTIF OF THE COYOTE. BE THAT AS IT MAY, SOMETIMES A RISTRA IS STILL REALLY A RISTRA.

(PAGES 70-71) ALBUQUERQUE'S PUBLIC ART RANGES FROM STYLIZED MURALS SUCH AS THIS COLORFUL DEPICTION OF COMMUNITY (ABOVE), PAINTED ON THE STREET-FACING SIDE OF A BACKSTOP IN MARTINEZTOWN, AND THIS BLACK-AND-WHITE, ALMOST PHOTO-REALISTIC HISTORIC SCENE (BELOW RIGHT) ON AN ADOBE WALL AT 12TH STREET AND MOUNTAIN ROAD, TO FOUND ART, SUCH AS THIS TINY GROCERY, ALSO IN MARTINEZTOWN (BELOW LEFT).

BERNALILLO COUNTY OFFERS AN AMAZING VARIETY OF LIFESTYLE CHOICES. THE SOUTH VALLEY IS A PLACE OF HORSES (ABOVE) AND LIVESTOCK PENS, IRRIGATION DITCHES, GREENHOUSES, HAY BARNS, AND AGRICULTURAL ACREAGE. MARY AND RONALD JOBE (RIGHT), ON TWO SOUTH VALLEY ACRES, KEEP CALVES, A SCORE OF CHICKENS, A TURKEY, MORE THAN FIFTY FRUIT TREES, AND DOZENS OF VARIETIES OF VEGETABLES—ALL WITHIN THE CITY LIMITS.

ON THE WEST SIDE, MEANWHILE, LUXURY HOMES REINTERPRET THE DETAILS AND TRADITIONS OF SOUTHWESTERN ARCHITECTURE ON BIG LOTS WITH COUNTRY CLUB FRONTAGES (BELOW). (FOLLOWING PAGES) THE FUTURE OF ALBUQUERQUE RESIDES IN THE HEARTS AND SPIRITS OF ITS YOUNG—LIKE LOUIE AND ANGELA, AS PROUD OF EACH OTHER AS OF LOUIE'S '64 IMPALA.

ALBUQUERQUE HAS COME A LONG WAY FROM ITS EARLY DAYS AS AN
ARCHITECTURALLY HOMOGENEOUS HAVEN OF PUEBLO STYLE ADOBE HOMES
AND CHURCHES. TODAY, IT IS ARCHITECTURALLY MANY THINGS: A CRADLE OF
AWARD-WINNING MODERN SOPHISTICATION, A PROVING GROUND FOR DARING
ARCHITECTURAL ADVENTURES, AND TRACTS OF HOMES THAT USE ELEMENTS
OF THE AREA'S INDIGENOUS STYLES AS STARTING POINTS FOR DESIGN.
INTERNATIONALLY RENOWNED ARCHITECT BART PRINCE MAKES HIS HOME
(LEFT) IN A STRIKING STRUCTURE RESEMBLING A SPACESHIP, WHILE THE
ARTISTIC WHIMSY OF THIS MOSAIC-FACED HOME (ABOVE) WAS DEEMED
REMARKABLE ENOUGH TO EARN A FEATURED SPOT IN *SMITHSONIAN* MAGAZINE.

Salmon and Mary Zamora (above right) live in the North Valley neighborhood where they both grew up—and in the very house where Salmon has lived most of his life. The city's rising economic tide has lifted many long-time Albuquerque families to a newfound prosperity; Salmon owns and runs an independent trucking company. Salmon can remember when their house had dirt floors, and while the neighbors have all left those behind, many of the homes retain charming traditional elements such as the adobe street walls (below right) that turn front yards into forecourt gardens. Those walls find their echo in pockets of town that preserve the picket fence Midwestern residentialism (above) that arrived in force with the railroad.

(Following pages) Older sections of Bernalillo County are still laced with *acequias*, or irrigation canals (left).

The hauntingly beautiful high-desert landscape is no longer much on display amidst the development of Albuquerque proper, but is still abundant on the east side of the Sandia Mountains (right), particularly on Sandia Crest Road, which leads up to the mountaintop.

Albuquerque is a community of exceptional people, from enterprising young businessman Julio Pordomo (above), owner and operator of the Discont (sic) Tire Shop, to Joanne Romero (right), a teacher at San Jose Elementary School, who tutors before school on her own time, coaches co-ed soccer in the afternoons, eats lunch with her students, gives them her home phone number, and serves on the executive board of the PTA and the school restructuring council (Photo by Eric O'Connell).

(Following pages) The village of Los Ranchos de Albuquerque is a place of spectacular homes and rustic landscape.

ALBUQUERQUEANS LOVE THE SPLENDOR OF THEIR NATURAL SURROUNDINGS
AND ARE DETERMINED THAT NO MANMADE STRUCTURES IMPEDE THEIR VIEWS.
THE BUILDINGS MAINTAIN A LOW PROFILE, WHICH LETS THE SANDIA MOUNTAINS
FUNCTION AS THE CITY'S SKYLINE ON ONE HORIZON AND THE VOLCANO CLIFFS
ON THE OTHER. BECAUSE OF THIS AND THE CITY'S ABUNDANCE OF OPEN SPACE,
ALBUQUERQUE HAS A DISTINCT FEELING OF EXPANSIVENESS.

Beyond Albuquerque's city limits lie a scattering of smaller communities offering everything from glimpses of the area's past to visions of its future. Corrales (above left) is a gorgeous combination of contemporary affluence and dirt road, old world quaintness. Rio Rancho (above), is an ingeniously successful planned community on the west side of the river.

Most neighborhoods aren't bordered by majestic mountains, but such is the case for residents of the Sandia foothills at the eastern edge of the city (below left). In addition to its beautiful open spaces, Placitas (below), lying just north of Albuquerque, is a mixture of older hispanic homes and newer luxury homes.

Nancy Kozikowski, weaver and painter, master of tapestry, works in collections from Albuquerque International Sunport to the Vatican (far left); Lorenzo Pimentel, hand-crafter of guitars (above).

TOP ROW: LINDA COTTON, ALBUQUERQUE'S FAVORITE CHANTEUSE; ANTOINE PREDOCK, INTERNATIONALLY RENOWNED ARCHITECT; STEPHEN HANKS, BRILLIANT WATERCOLORIST, NATIONAL WATERCOLOR SOCIETY MERIT AWARD WINNER 1991, NATIONAL ACADEMY OF WESTERN ART GOLD MEDAL IN WATERCOLOR WINNER 1992, DECLARED ONE OF AMERICA'S TOP 10 MOST COLLECTED AND COLLECTABLE ARTISTS BY US ART MAGAZINE 1993; FLOYD CORREA, PRESIDENT AND OWNER, CORREA ENTERPRISES, SOFTWARE DESIGN, FORMER GOVERNOR, LAGUNA PUEBLO; BILL DAILY, FILM AND TELEVISION ACTOR (I DREAM OF JEANNIE), COMIC, THEATER DIRECTOR.

CENTER ROW: DANNY ROMERO, BOXING CHAMPION; JIM WALL, PRESIDENT, AMREP SOUTHWEST; FRED WILSON, POTTER, MUDDY WHEEL POTTERY; SID GUTIERREZ, SPACE SHUTTLE ASTRONAUT; COLONEL ELIZABETH ANN HARRELL, COMMANDER, 377TH AIR BASE WING, KIRTLAND AIR FORCE BASE; PABLITA VELARDE, RENOWNED NATIVE AMERICAN ARTIST.

BOTTOM ROW: KEN ENGLADE, BEST-SELLING AUTHOR, TRUE-CRIME SPECIALIST; BART PRINCE, PEERLESS ARCHITECT, FEARLESS DESIGNER; SYLVIA ORTIZ, CLOTHING DESIGNER; JOSEPH POWDRELL, FOUNDER AND OWNER, POWDRELL'S BARBECUE; ROBERTA COOPER RAMO, ATTORNEY, FIRST FEMALE PRESIDENT, AMERICAN BAR ASSOCIATION; EILEEN WELSOME, INVESTIGATIVE JOURNALIST, WINNER OF PULITZER PRIZE, 1994.

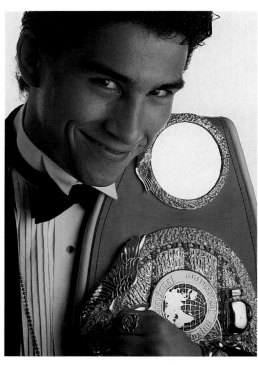

(PREVIOUS PAGES) AS THE RIO GRANDE, WHICH RISES IN THE SAN JUAN
MOUNTAINS IN SOUTHWESTERN COLORADO AND MAKES A NEARLY 2,000-MILE
RUN TO THE GULF OF MEXICO, PASSES THROUGH ALBUQUERQUE, IT DISPLAYS
A SURPRISINGLY RETIRING PERSONALITY, FLOWING SEDATELY BETWEEN BANKS
LUSHLY FORESTED WITH COTTONWOOD TREES AND SERVING AS A SWEEPING
RECREATIONAL RESOURCE FOR WATER ENTHUSIASTS OF EVERY STRIPE—LIKE
THESE COMBERS AND DOG-WALKERS WHO HAVE SPLASHED OUT TO A SANDBAR
JUST NORTH OF THE BARELAS BRIDGE.

THE SANDIAS ARE A SPECTACULARLY LOVELY BACKDROP AND A PEERLESS
RECREATIONAL VENUE IN ANY SEASON (ABOVE AND PAGES 98-99), BUT IN
WINTER, THE STARK, HEART-STOPPING BEAUTY OF THE WIND-WHIPPED PEAK
(LEFT) COMES AT A PRICE FOR SIGHTSEERS: THE SITE CAN BE ICY AND VERY
FRIGID— ABOUT 30° COLDER THAN THE CITY PROPER, COLDER STILL WITH
WIND CHILL.

(PAGES 100-101) ANOTHER OF ALBUQUERQUE'S REMARKABLE NATURAL
FEATURES IS THE LIGHT. IT MAKES FOR SPECTACULAR DAWNS, INDESCRIBABLE
SKY- AND LIGHTSCAPES, AND EXQUISITE SUNSETS.
AS BEFITS AN AREA LARGELY SETTLED BY ROMAN CATHOLICS, THE REGION IS
RICH IN HISTORIC CATHOLIC CHURCHES. AT THE VERY HEART OF OLD TOWN,
SAN FELIPE DE NERI (LEFT AND ABOVE) DATES BACK TO 1793 (IT REPLACED
AN OLDER CHURCH BUILT IN 1706) AND STILL HOLDS REGULAR SERVICES.
IN MARTINEZTOWN, SAN YGNACIO (PAGE 104) IS MUCH MORE THAN THE
RELIGIOUS CENTER OF ITS COMMUNITY, WHILE THE MUD-WALLED OLD
CORRALES CHURCH (PAGE 105) HAS BEEN REPLACED (BY THE NEW CORRALES
CHURCH) AND IS NOW A COMMUNITY ACTIVITIES CENTER.

HISTORIC SPLENDOR TO ONE SIDE, PERHAPS THE MOST SPECTACULAR CHURCH
IN TOWN IS HOFFMANTOWN BAPTIST (ABOVE LEFT, OPPOSITE - PHOTO BY
DOUGLAS MERRIAM), WHICH COST $11 MILLION TO BUILD IN 1987. THE
CHURCH BOASTS SOME 10,000 MEMBERS.

ALBUQUERQUE'S TRADITION OF FAITH IS MANIFEST OUTSIDE CHURCHES AS
WELL—IN WARES AT THE WEEKLY FLEA MARKET (ABOVE); MURALS
THROUGHOUT TOWN (ABOVE RIGHT, OPPOSITE); THE TRADITION OF THE
SANTO, A RELIGIOUS WOODEN CARVING (BELOW RIGHT, OPPOSITE) THAT TODAY
IS SOMETHING OF A HYBRID OF ICON AND ARTWORK; AND LIFELONG DEVOTION
TO THE CHURCH AS A SERVANT OF GOD (BELOW LEFT, OPPOSITE - PHOTO BY
ERIC O'CONNELL).

THE ROOF OF CONGREGATION B'NAI ISRAEL (ABOVE LEFT), ONE OF
ALBUQUERQUE'S TWO FLOURISHING SYNAGOGUES, PRESENTS A BROAD,
TENT-LIKE SHELTER FOR THE CITY'S JEWISH FAITHFUL—WHO, BY THEIR OWN
ESTIMATE, MAKE UP ONLY 1.5% OF ALBUQUERQUE'S POPULATION.
WAT BUDDHAMONGKOLNIMIT, A LAOTIAN THERAVADA BUDDHIST MONASTERY
(ABOVE - PHOTO BY DOUGLAS MERRIAM) AND THE NEWEST BUDDHIST TEMPLE
IN ALBUQUERQUE, IS HOME TO MONKS WHO HAVE GRADUATED FROM THE
BUDDHIST UNIVERSITY IN BANGKOK.

(PREVIOUS PAGES) THERE ARE THOSE WHO BEST ENJOY THE MOUNTAINS BY
LEAPING FROM THEIR PEAKS, AND ALBUQUERQUE IS THEIR PLAYGROUND FOR
ALL SORTS OF AERIAL ADVENTURES, FROM HANG GLIDING, SKYDIVING, AND
PARAGLIDING TO, OF COURSE, BALLOONING.

FOR OTHERS, THE ENJOYMENT COMES IN THE MULTITUDE OF WAYS OF GET-
TING UP INTO THE MOUNTAINS. ONE OF THE MOST POPULAR POINTS OF ENTRY
IS THE ELENA GALLEGOS PICNIC AREA, LOCATED WITHIN ALBERT G. SIMMS
PARK AT THE IMMEDIATE BASE OF THE RANGE. FROM ELENA GALLEGOS,
VISITORS CAN HIKE (ABOVE LEFT) OR BIKE IN AND CONNECT WITH AN EXTEN-
SIVE NETWORK OF TRAILS LACING THE MOUNTAINS.

OFFERING THE SPECTACULAR SCENERY WITH NONE OF THE EXERTION, THE
SANDIA PEAK AERIAL TRAMWAY (ABOVE) SOARS 4,000 FEET OVER A DISTANCE
OF 2.7 MILES IN LESS THAN 20 MINUTES. RUNNING YEAR-ROUND (EXCEPT
DURING HIGH WINDS), THE TRAM IS ONE OF THE ATTRACTIONS *EVERYONE*
RECOMMENDS—BOTH FOR THE DRAMA OF THE JOURNEY AND FOR THE
BREATHTAKING VIEW FROM THE SUMMIT.

AT 10,000 FEET, THE SANDIA PEAK SKI AREA OFFERS COLD, CLEAR AIR AND HUNDRED-MILE VISTAS—AS WELL AS FAMILY-ORIENTED SKIING ON AN ARRAY OF DOWNHILL (ABOVE - PHOTO BY JAY BLACKWOOD) AND NORDIC TRAILS. IN THE WARMER MONTHS MOUNTAIN BIKERS GET THEIR KICKS NEGOTIATING THE MOUNTAIN'S EIGHT TRAILS, RANGING FROM EASY TO DIFFICULT. DURING SUMMER AND FALL, THE PEAK RUNS ONE OF ITS LIFTS AS A SIGHTSEEING ATTRACTION, TAKING VISITORS TO THE PEAK VISTA POINT THROUGH STANDS OF PINES AND ASPENS. TAKING THE LIFT GIVES RIDERS THE CHANCE TO ENJOY THE CRISP MOUNTAIN AIR, THE SMELL OF THE TREES, AND, IN FALL, THE SPECTACULAR TURNING OF THE ASPEN LEAVES.

Outdoor enthusiasts love Albuquerque's climate. Not only does the region offer the unique possibility of skiing and golfing in the same day—and with very little driving time in between—but many of the golf courses, such as the Rio Rancho Country Club (above), also offer breathtaking scenery.

ALBUQUERQUE'S MANY SUN WORSHIPPERS LOVE THE CITY'S SUMMERS, WHEN TEMPERATURES RISE INTO THE 90S AND STRETCHES OF 100° AREN'T UNCOMMON. IT IS IN PART THE SUN THAT BRINGS THEM OUT FOR THE DAY-LONG 4TH OF JULY CELEBRATION AT KIRTLAND AIR FORCE BASE — ALTHOUGH IT'S ALSO IN PART THE LIVE MUSIC, THE AIRSHOW, AND THE DAZZLING FIREWORKS DISPLAY (LEFT).

BUT IT IS AFTER THE SUN GOES DOWN, WHEN THE AIR COOLS AND THE LIGHT IS JUST RIGHT, THAT ALBUQUERQUE MAY WELL BE AT ITS BEST. EVEN CASUAL BASEBALL FANS REGULARLY ATTEND ALBUQUERQUE DUKES HOME GAMES (ABOVE). AAA FARM TEAM FOR THE LOS ANGELES DODGERS, THE DUKES HAVE A WAY OF PLAYING THAT TURNS CASUAL FANS INTO UNSHAKABLE ENTHUSIASTS. AND SUMMER IS SHOW TIME, TOO, FOR ALBUQUERQUE LITTLE LEAGUERS WITH DREAMS OF BECOMING BIG LEAGUERS (BELOW).

Emack
&
Bolio's

ROUTE
66

ROUTE
66

ICE CREAM·YOGURT·COFFEE

3001

OPEN

(Pages 124-125) Not all the city's murals find their purpose in profundity. Some, like this one in Nob Hill, simply harken back to a golden age of Albuquerque's pivotal role in national migration. (Photo by Douglas Merriam)

(Pages 126-127) If the city's avant-garde has a geographical center, it is Nob Hill, where, among many other delectable shops, restaurants, and businesses, Emack & Bolio's (left) and Il Vicino (right) explore the gourmet possibilities of ice cream and pizza, respectively. (Photos by Douglas Merriam)

But Albuquerque shows equal appreciation for the venerable—such as the 66 Diner (above left), a world-renowned and widely beloved purveyor of out-of-this-world burger-fries-shake combos as well as home-style favorites like hash and meatloaf, all served out of the former home of Sam's 66 Service station, built in 1946. (Sadly, 66 Diner was gutted by fire in 1995 and razed. But the owners rebuilt, replicating as much of the original building as they could.) And

patrons of the Owl Cafe (below left) celebrate the institution of the roadside diner as only New Mexico could create it—with green chile on everything. This Owl is a city cousin to the original, which lies about 100 miles south in tiny San Antonio and was reputedly a favorite stop of the atomic bomb engineers, who tested their creation several miles east of the little town. For those seeking mouth-watering preparations of favorite New Mexican dishes, Garcia's (above) boasts an irresistibly unassuming air, decor redolent of the founder and owner's background in novelty sales, and food that dreams are made of.

(Following pages) Metropolitan Albuquerque is also cosmopolitan Albuquerque, and Mexican and New Mexican aren't the only cuisines that receive stamps of authenticity and approval. Ta Lin is an authentic Asian grocery and one of the city's truly great food markets. (Photo by Douglas Merriam)

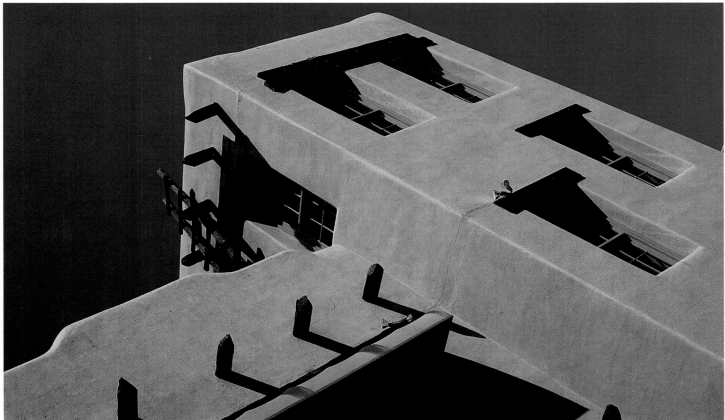

THE SKY THAT LIFTS FOREVER ABOVE THE REGION IS UNFAILINGLY AMAZING. LOOK UP AND YOU'LL SEE INSTANTLY HOW RIGHT WILLA CATHER WAS IN HER NOVEL OF NEW MEXICO, *DEATH COMES FOR THE ARCHBISHOP*, WHEN SHE WROTE, "ELSEWHERE THE SKY IS THE ROOF OF THE WORLD; BUT HERE THE EARTH WAS THE FLOOR OF THE SKY." THE SKY HAS INSPIRED A CERTAIN VERTICALITY IN SOME OF THE URBAN AND INDUSTRIAL DESIGN IN THE CITY, WHERE PROPRIETORS HAVE REACHED UP INTO IT WITH THEIR SIGNS AND THEIR BUILDINGS: THE ARCHING SUPERSTRUCTURE AT HOFFMANTOWN SHOPPING CENTER (ABOVE LEFT), THE NEON-ENHANCED FACE CARD AT JACK'S LIQUOR STORE (ABOVE), THE FIRE-TOWER FACADE OF MONTE VISTA FIRE STATION (BELOW), AND THE CANDY CANE AT BUFFETT'S CANDIES FACTORY AND STORE (BELOW LEFT).

MARKING THE NOB HILL DISTRICT LESS FORMALLY THAN THE NEON PUBLIC-ART ARCHES—IF MORE FAMILIARLY FOR GENERATIONS OF ALBUQUERQUEANS—IS THE LOBO THEATER (LEFT), A CLASSIC MOVIE PALACE BELOVED BY STUDENTS FROM THE UNIVERSITY OF NEW MEXICO TWO BLOCKS WEST. IN ADDITION TO ITS REGULAR TRIPLE-BILL LINEUP OF SECOND- AND THIRD-RUN FEATURES AND MIDNIGHT SHOWS, THE THEATER ORGANIZES AND HOSTS THE ANNUAL BORDERLANDS FILM FESTIVAL, THE ONLY FILM FESTIVAL IN THE NATION DEVOTED EXCLUSIVELY TO MEXICAN FINE-ART CINEMA .

IN SUMMER, CIVIC PLAZA DOWNTOWN COMES ALIVE (ABOVE) WITH JAM-PACKED SUMMERFEST CELEBRATIONS. EACH WEEK THE FOOD, MUSIC AND HANDICRAFTS OF DIFFERENT CULTURES ARE FEATURED.

(FOLLOWING PAGES) HARKENING BACK TO A BYGONE ERA, THE ALBUQUERQUE 6 DRIVE-IN SUPPLEMENTED ITS ROSTER OF FIRST-RUN FILMS WITH UNOBSTRUCTED VIEWS OF THE CITY'S AWE-INSPIRING SUMMER SUNSETS AND EVENING SKIES—A COMBINATION THAT MADE GOING TO THE MOVIES AN ALMOST RELIGIOUS EXPERIENCE UNTIL RECENTLY, WHEN THE THEATER WAS SCHEDULED FOR DEMOLITION TO MAKE WAY FOR AN INDOOR MULTIPLEX.

ALBUQUERQUE AND BERNALILLO COUNTY PRIDE THEMSELVES ON BEING A
REGION WITH PLENTY TO OFFER ITS YOUNGER DENIZENS. THE ALBUQUERQUE
CHILDREN'S MUSEUM (ABOVE) SUCCESSFULLY MIXES EDUCATION AND PLAY IN
A WIDE-RANGING SERIES OF IMAGINATIVE HANDS-ON EXHIBITS.

BESPEAKING A PERIOD OF LOWER TECH AND GREATER INNOCENCE, THE
RAINBOW GARDEN ROLLER DROME (ABOVE LEFT) LAYS CLAIM TO THE
DISTINCTION OF BEING THE LARGEST MAPLE-FLOOR ROLLER RINK IN THE
WORLD. IT ALSO HAS A LARGE SECOND RINK FOR BEGINNERS WHO DON'T WANT
TO BRAVE THE MAIN FLOOR.

AND THE CITY'S MAMMOTH WEEKLY FLEA MARKET IS ONE OF THE BIGGEST IN
THE NATION—A SPRAWLING AMERICAN BAZAAR THAT IS PART GARAGE SALE,
PART ARTS-AND-CRAFTS FAIR, PART ANTIQUES BOUTIQUE, PART JUNKYARD, PART
MIRACLE-PRODUCT SHOWCASE, AND PART HUSTLE (BELOW LEFT). OPEN IN
THE EXPANSIVE PARKING LOT AT THE STATE FAIRGROUNDS VIRTUALLY YEAR-
ROUND (ONLY SNOW AND THE STATE FAIR CLOSE IT DOWN), THE FLEA MARKET
IS ARGUABLY THE BEST PLACE IN TOWN FOR EVERYTHING FROM SURPLUS TRAFFIC
LIGHTS TO DEFUNCT ELECTRIC BROOMS, FRESH-PICKED CHILES TO FUZZY
DICE, PYREX COFFEE POTS TO SUN-WRACKED PAPERBACKS, COLLECTIBLE (AND
NOT-SO-COLLECTIBLE) CURIOS TO REMAINDERED RELIGIOUS ITEMS.

(FOLLOWING PAGES) DIFFICULT TO DESCRIBE, IMPOSSIBLE TO FORGET, THE
TINKERTOWN MUSEUM IS A MUST-SEE FOR ANYONE INTERESTED IN THAT
PECULIAR CLASS OF AMERICANA, THE ROADSIDE ATTRACTION—GIANT BALLS
OF STRING, MUMMIFIED ALIENS, AND MAGIC OR "IT" SPOTS. TINKERTOWN IS A
SHOWCASE OF GENUINE ARTISTRY—EXPANSIVE SCALE MODELS OF, AMONG
OTHER THINGS, AN OLD WEST TOWN AND A THREE-RING CIRCUS, ALL
COMPOSED ENTIRELY OF HAND-CARVED MINIATURE FIGURES.

(PAGES 142-143) NEAR THE BAND SHELL AT THE CITY ZOO, A POND IS HOME
TO GOLDEN KOI—ONE OF THE LESS EXOTIC SPECIES ON DISPLAY.

A GRAB BAG OF SIGHTS AND SITES AROUND THE CITY (LEFT TO RIGHT, TOP TO BOTTOM): SANDIA SHADOWS WINERY, LOCATED…WELL, IN THE SHADOW OF THE SANDIAS; *WALK IN BEAUTY*, 1983 SCULPTURE BY DOUG HYDE AT THE ALBUQUERQUE MUSEUM; AN OFFER NO RESIDENT COULD REFUSE; MIDNIGHT RODEO, THE CITY'S SURREAL TEMPLE OF LINE-DANCING AND COUNTRY-WESTERN WORSHIP; MOVIE WORLD, A MURAL ON THE WALL OF A VIDEO SHOP, THE CREATION OF JOE STEPHENSON, M. "CRASH" BELTRAN, AND STUDENTS FROM WASHINGTON MIDDLE SCHOOL; A GENUINE B-52 BOMBER ON DISPLAY AT THE NATIONAL ATOMIC MUSEUM; A NEW MEXICO SYMPHONY ORCHESTRA CONCERT IN THE BAND SHELL AT THE ZOO; TWO GENERATIONS OF HATS; A BIG CAT TAKING A BIG NAP AT THE RIO GRANDE ZOOLOGICAL PARK; A SOUTH VALLEY AUTOSHOP ADVERTISES ITS SPECIALTY; DESERT FLORA; ONE OF THE STARS OF THE FULL-SCALE, WALK-THROUGH DINOSAUR DIORAMA AT THE NEW MEXICO MUSEUM OF NATURAL HISTORY; THE BEACH WATERPARK, A VAST WATER PARK IN LANDLOCKED ALBUQUERQUE WITH TWO HEATED WAVE POOLS (ONE WITH SMALLER WAVES FOR SMALLER KIDS), SLIDES, AND A RIVER.

PROFILES OF SUCCESS

THE CORPORATIONS, BUSINESS ORGANIZATIONS AND EDUCATIONAL INSTITUTIONS WHICH FOLLOW REPRESENT THE REGION'S THRIVING AND DIVERSE BUSINESS COMMUNITY. THEIR PROFILES HELP TELL THE STORY OF ALBUQUERQUE AND BERNALILLO COUNTY.

PHOTOGRAPHY BY JERRY RABINOWITZ
PROFILES WRITTEN BY MICHAEL BAWAYA
PRODUCTION DIRECTOR DAPHNE DOBECKI
PROFILE MANAGER SARA CROSSMAN
CORPORATE LIAISON JOHN GARCIA
(EXCEPT AS NOTED)

Albuquerque Convention and Visitors Bureau

The Albuquerque Convention and Visitors Bureau (ACVB) is the foremost expert regarding conventions and tourism in New Mexico. It has earned this status by furnishing a variety of essential services and possessing a wealth of information.

The ACVB was conceived as a department of the Albuquerque Chamber of Commerce. In December of 1980, it was incorporated by the board of directors as a private, nonprofit association and was awarded a

The ACVB plays an important role in the community's economic development

contract by the City of Albuquerque for convention and tourism promotion.

The ACVB's success is a result of the combined efforts of its extensive membership, which include hotels, airlines, restaurants, tour operators, transportation companies, professional services, retail establishments, and other representatives of the community. These members elect a board of directors, which in turn names an executive committee of twelve members who work with the president/CEO to assure the board's policies are carried out.

The bureau's Tourism Division attracts visitors to Albuquerque and guides them to member businesses. The Tourism Division has dramatically increased the number of visitor inquiries and

trade contacts, which are approaching 200,000. This division also creates a number of free publications, such as the *Albuquerque Visitor's Guide, Thirty Ways For Kids To Have Fun In Albuquerque,* and *The Art of Accessibility*, which address families, children and also travelers with disabilities. The bureau's three visitor centers, located at

Above: The ACVB provides visitors with all the information they need to make the most of their trip.

Below: Richard Gilliland, ACVB's President and CEO.

formed the Albuquerque Sports Council, a division that brings various sporting events to the city. These achievements only begin to measure the bureau's impact on the community. Travel/tourism is a $1.6 billion a year industry here — conventions alone generated $295 million — supporting 16,000 jobs. Nearly 2,000 hotel rooms are being added to the local market, and the expansion of the Albuquerque Convention Center and a skyrocketing

Albuquerque has become a major tourist destination.

the airport, Downtown and Old Town, have knowledgeable staff who are familiar with both the city's popular and lesser known attractions and establishments.

"There are several factors why the Albuquerque Convention and Visitors Bureau is so important to the economic development of our community," observes Richard Gilliland, the bureau's President and CEO. "The convention and meetings' market generates $75 billion and 1.5 billion jobs in the United States. Twenty-three percent of all airline business comes from the convention and meeting trade."

The bureau's Convention Sales Division, dubbed the A-Team for their many successes, has booked hundreds of conventions over the last few years, the revenues from which generally exceed $100 million annually. This division is funded exclusively by receipts from the city's Lodger Tax, and these tax dollars are well spent. One year, for example, $1.5 million worth of tax receipts resulted in the A-Team booking more than $160 million in future convention business, an incredible return on investment.

America Japan Week New Mexico, coordinated by the bureau, was the largest cultural exchange in the state's history. The ACVB created ¡Magnifico! Festival of the Arts, an annual, nine day celebration of the visual arts which attracts visitors. The bureau also

number of visitor inquiries are just a few signs that the hospitality industry continues to rise. The ACVB is largely responsible for this.

Guaranteeing that conventions run smoothly is the task of the Bureau Services Division. They've proven they're equal to the task, having twice earned the prestigious Gold Service Award from the industry's top trade publication, *Meetings and Conventions* magazine.

Though it's won some of the convention and visitor industry's top awards, the bureau continually strives to improve.

"There is no way to emphasize that service is the most critical ingredient in securing bureau business," Gilliland avers. "No matter what we have to offer, and no matter how well the bureau staff tries to sell it, the bottom line is how well our members and the hospitality community service our customers."

In addition to its other endeavors, the ACVB participates in numerous community activities, supporting the Albuquerque Chamber of Commerce, Albuquerque Hispano Chamber of Commerce, Rio Grande Minority Purchasing Council, Albuquerque Economic Development and other nonprofit organizations. The bureau has also conducted fund raisers and clothing drives for various crisis shelters. ▟

Albuquerque Economic Development, Inc.

It is necessary, in a growing city like Albuquerque, to broaden the economic base and create new job opportunities so that citizens can enjoy a healthy, stable and balanced economy. This is the purpose of Albuquerque Economic Development, Inc. (AED), a private, nonprofit membership corporation.

"To date," explains Chairman Larry Willard, "AED has recruited more than 175 businesses to the city, providing more than 20,000 direct jobs for area residents and hundreds of millions of payroll dollars."

Back in the 1950s the Greater Albuquerque Chamber of Commerce, recognizing the need to recruit new businesses to diversify the economy, formed an industrial development committee. In 1960, members of this committee and the chamber board approved a plan leading to the creation of the Albuquerque Industrial Development Services, which, in 1986, became Albuquerque Economic Development, Inc.

The main goal of AED is to attract new manufacturing, research and development, and other businesses from outside of New Mexico to Albuquerque. A limited number of companies relocate each year, and Albuquerque competes against other cities that are equally intent on having these companies. Through the use of effective marketing programs, an array of services and a can-do attitude, AED succeeds in drawing businesses here and facilitates their relocation and expansion.

"AED's priority has been to create quality jobs for our quality workers," explains AED's Chairman Larry Willard. "To date, AED has recruited more than 175 businesses to the city, providing more than 20,000 direct jobs for area residents and hundreds of millions of payroll dollars. It is difficult to point to

Sumitomo Sitix Silicon, Motorola and Southwest Airlines are among the major corporations that AED helped bring to Albuquerque.

another force in the community which has so broad an impact."

AED works with state and local governments, other economic development organizations with similar objectives and values, and the business community. It seeks to benefit both Albuquerque and the businesses that move here. AED was instrumental in persuading such illustrious corporations as General Mills, Honeywell, Intel, Baxter Healthcare, Olympus,

Philips Semiconductors, MCI Services Marketing, Sumitomo Sitix Silicon, and Southwest Airlines to join the local business community. It also played an important role in the multibillion dollar expansion of Intel.

Two vital and growing components of the city's economy are the high-tech and biomed/biotech industries, which AED cultivates. With the University of New Mexico, Albuquerque Technical Vocational Institute, Sandia National Laboratories and the Air Force's Phillips Laboratory located here, and Los Alamos National Laboratory nearby, Albuquerque possesses an impressive pool of scientists, researchers and skilled technical workers capable of providing highly specialized technical assistance to new businesses.

To illustrate the several advantages of Albuquerque, AED provides a wide range of information and data including site surveys and wage comparisons. It offers counsel on funding sources and incentive programs such as industrial revenue bonds, and serves as a liaison between businesses and government agencies to assist with regulations and permits.

By advertising in trade and business publications and attending industry trade shows, AED promotes the community. It also employs a public relations program that disseminates news about Albuquerque to business editors and reporters, and publishes brochures and other materials concerning the local economy, such as the *Albuquerque Directory of Manufacturers*. This aggressive promotion has resulted in some forty articles appearing in national publications in recent years. *Money* magazine selected Albuquerque as one of the ten "Best Places to Live in America,"and *U.S. News & World Report* rated it one of the country's seven "Great Places to Live." *Entrepreneur* saluted the city for being one of the "Top 20 U.S. Business Locations."

AED is governed by a board of directors representing the business community, and ex officio members from governmental and educational institutions.

"New companies to the Albuquerque area give hope and employment to our citizens, generate tax revenues for our schools and other social programs and create payroll that will be spent on housing, food and shopping," Willard adds. "A new company and its employees fund charities, churches and organizations of all kinds and produce an economic multiplier which creates other jobs as it ripples through the community."

Albuquerque Hispano Chamber of Commerce

Albuquerque is known for its multiculturalism. Approximately 37% of the residents are of Hispanic heritage and they have in many ways influenced the city's culture over a period of more than 500 years.

While international trade, conventions and tourism and other large scale endeavors have been important activities of the AHCC, perhaps its most significant contribution is assisting small businesses.

ALBUQUERQUE
NEW MEXICO, U.S.A.

ALBUQUERQUE HISPANO CHAMBER of COMMERCE

The business world is another place where the city's Hispanic citizenry have made their mark, thanks in part to the Albuquerque Hispano Chamber of Commerce (AHCC), which plays a vital role in the business community by promoting economic and educational opportunities and dedicating itself to making Albuquerque a better place.

The AHCC offers a variety of services including marketing assistance, no-fee business consultations, business referrals, and workshops and seminars. It also distributes *At A Glance*, its monthly newsletter.

There are only a few chambers of commerce which possess a Convention and Tourism department, and the AHCC is one of them. In 1977, the Albuquerque City Council decided that the AHCC was an ideal organization for promoting tourism. The City Council assigned it the task of attracting local, national and international conventions to Albuquerque. Gladly accepting this assignment, the AHCC has been extremely successful, having, in a recent year, generated more than $18 million for the city. Due to such extraordinary efforts they have been designated one of the top convention and tourism departments in the country by the United States Travel and Tourism Association.

Another focal point of the

AHCC is initiating international trade. The organization spearheaded several international meetings, alliances and conferences, such as the First Annual Mexican Trade Summit, held in 1992, and the Camino Real Economic Alliance, an international

Above:

The significance of the Hispanic contribution to the settlement of Albuquerque is represented here by a composite view of Old Town. The statue of Don Francisco y Valdez, founder of Albuquerque, is located north of the plaza.

Below: The AHCC's Board of Directors.

$70,000 in scholarship funds to local Hispanic students in 1995. It also cosponsors, along with the City of Albuquerque and Intel Corporation, a Stay-in-School program for urban high school students, and its school-to-work program CHOICES was awarded a grant from the U.S. Department of Education.

"There are a lot of expectations of us from the community locally, regionally and nationally," observes Chairman Ruth Alicia Ruiz.

Though the expectations are high, the AHCC is more than capable of meeting them. A strategic plan for the future is in place which includes a move to larger quarters and a new logo. To help implement this plan, Dr. Ronald Chavez has assumed the position of President.

The AHCC has the confidence that comes from having been twice honored - in 1986 and 1990 - as United States Hispanic Chamber of the Year, chosen from a field of

The Executive Committee of the AHCC.

business networking organization, created in 1993.

The AHCC can boast of having played a role in the founding of numerous local organizations, among them the Small Business Resource Mercado and the New Mexico Hispanic Cultural Center.

While international trade, conventions and tourism and other large scale endeavors have been important activities of the AHCC, perhaps its most significant contribution is assisting small businesses. Certified as a Small Business Resource Center, the AHCC helps new companies get on their feet. Small businesses, professional companies, and numerous high-tech and corporate entities can all thank the AHCC for seed money and good advice. Loan packaging and technical and management assistance are available to its members at no cost. In addition, AHCC awarded

more than 250 Hispanic chambers of commerce. It is one of the largest Hispanic chambers as well, with more than 1150 members. The AHCC Annual Banquet is the biggest in the Southwest, with more than 2,000 attendees, a number of whom come from out of state. This event has become such a success that other organizations, such as the National Hispanic Bankers Association, have scheduled important meetings in Albuquerque to coincide with the banquet.

Back in 1975, when the AHCC was conceived by thirteen business people, its founders chose the motto "Membership Means Business" to represent the spirit of the organization. Its many activities are proof that the AHCC continues to mean business today.

Bernalillo County

The origins of Bernalillo County date back to Mexican rule, when two partidos, or districts, were created here in 1837. Further subdivisions followed, and the territory was later annexed by the United States. It was formally incorporated as a county in 1912, the same year New Mexico attained statehood.

Since its inception, the county has been a guiding force for progress in New Mexico. With Albuquerque

Since its inception in 1912, the county has been a guiding force for progress in New Mexico—and a pioneering leader in resident service.

as its focal point, Bernalillo County has established itself as a statewide center of industry, commerce, and culture. It encompasses over 1,168 square miles and has a population of 518,031.

The county derives its authority from the state constitution and has a Commission/Manager form of government. It is divided into five commission districts. The County Manager serves as the chief administrator of 25 departments, a 1,300-member work force, and an annual budget of roughly $105 million. Its citizens elect five other officials to carry out statutory responsibilities: the County Assessor, County Clerk, Probate Judge, Treasurer and Sheriff.

Bernalillo County provides New Mexico's most comprehensive and progressive system of local government services. In conjunction with the City of Albuquerque, it offers residents access to GOV 14, a local government TV station, as well as computerized access to important government information. There are currently over fifty joint power agreements in place between the city and the county, the most significant being the joint operation of the adult detention center, with a budget of nearly $22 million, and the joint operation of a regional library system, with fifteen branch

Gamelsky Benton Architects, P.C.

locations throughout the area.

Bernalillo County has constitutional responsibility for conducting elections, performing property assessments, tax collection, and the recording and maintaining of many official documents. Unlike many other counties, Bernalillo provides such services as housing, building planning and zoning, and parks and recreation.

Public Works is one of the largest divisions in the county, employing over 100 workers and administering nearly $15 million in federal and state highway funds in addition to county general fund monies.

Ross Romero, Bernalillo County Public Information Office

Above: East Mountain Library is one of fifteen branch locations within the county.

Below: The land for this North Valley soccer field, donated by a private citizen, contributes to the quality of life in Bernalillo County.

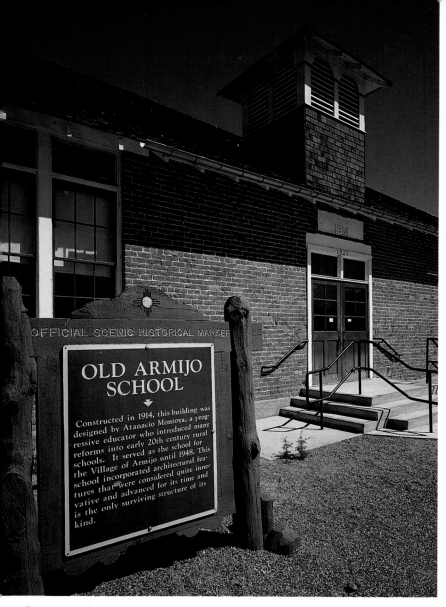

OFFICIAL SCENIC HISTORICAL MARKER

OLD ARMIJO SCHOOL

Constructed in 1914, this building was designed by Atanacio Montoya, a progressive educator who introduced many reforms into early 20th century rural schools. It served as the school for the Village of Armijo until 1948. This school incorporated architectural features that were considered quite innovative and advanced for its time and is the only surviving structure of its kind.

imposes impact fees on new development to generate revenues for new parks and open space, drainage system improvement, fire fighting equipment, and streets.

The Housing Department administers an annual budget of more than $8 million, providing rental assistance and housing renovation services to over 700 families. Sixty-one county owned housing units provide homes for low income, physically disabled, and elderly residents.

Citizens of all ages benefit from a wide range of recreational, leisure, and educational opportunities offered at six community centers and three senior centers. The 237 acres maintained by the Parks Department in the county's unincorporated areas contain 16 parks and a like number of mini-parks, 11 softball fields, 4 pools, 10 soccer fields, 27 tennis courts, and 23 little league fields.

Bernalillo County restored the Old Armijo School, which is now a community center used for public meetings and social services programs.

Engineers plan and design major traffic arterials, drainage systems, water supply systems, and sewer lines for county residents.

The county's Public Safety Division includes one of the largest fire and rescue operations in the state, staffed by both paid and volunteer fire fighters and paramedics.

Bernalillo County operates a Juvenile Detention Center which handles over 3,000 high risk juveniles annually. The John E. Brown Juvenile Justice Complex deals with probation, court proceedings, and legally required counseling services for all juvenile cases in the metropolitan area.

Bernalillo County's Environmental Health Department administers a variety of programs to protect the public health and provide assistance for low income residents. This includes financial assistance for safe drinking water and sewage disposal systems for their homes.

The county's zoning system ensures that new development occurs in an orderly, sustainable, and environmentally sensitive manner. The county also

"Bernalillo County's independent 1995 financial audit had no negative findings and only minor recommendations for improvements," says County Manager Juan Vigil. This achievement and the county's overall financial stability resulted in AA bond ratings from both Moody's and Standard & Poor's for its first revenue bond issue. Bernalillo County is one of only two counties nationally to receive such high bond ratings.

Bernalillo County Government goes far beyond the basic mandates for road maintenance, tax collection, and law enforcement. The County Commission deals regularly with critical issues affecting the economy and lifestyles of citizens throughout the region and state.

Bernalillo County Government is professionally managed and fiscally sound. It continues to make great strides in meeting the needs of a dynamic and ever growing population.

City of Albuquerque

Albuquerque is a growing city of great achievements and ambitions.

The city's economy, for example, is booming. It regularly outperforms the rest of the country in job growth, with employment in the metropolitan statistical area increasing every year since 1961. In 1994, the city added more than 17,000 jobs.

Although the star players in the economy are high-tech manufacturers and their suppliers, a growing

Albuquerque is dedicated to providing its residents and its businesses with "safe, attractive neighborhoods, good schools, and clean air and water."

service sector and a strong tourism and convention industry are also making a contribution.

"Albuquerque welcomes economic development and job growth that improves the quality of life for its residents," states Mayor Martin J. Chávez.

This philosophy is supported by an active airport, a strong capital improvements program, and the Office of Economic Development, all of which work together to further business development and growth. Industrial revenue bonds are available for large businesses, while smaller companies may take advantage of direct loan or loan guarantee programs. Technical support and job training services are also available. On-line information can be accessed concerning city purchasing requirements and opportunities.

"I was born and raised here and I love Albuquerque," says Chávez. "I want high-paying jobs so our kids can have a wonderful future here."

The Chávez administration has brought about a number of innovations, including:

— An Economic Development Strategy, which stresses ongoing collaboration among businesses, non-profit groups, and local government.

— A community policing policy that puts officers in direct contact with the community, allowing them to team with neighborhood associations, residents, and businesses to create a safe environment. Public safety is a top priority of the Chávez administration.

—The Mayor's Council on Gangs, which seeks innovative ways to combat gangs, such as supporting middle-school sports programs.

—The Office of Anti-Graffiti Coordination, which operates a hot line (857-8055) citizens can call to report graffiti and also sponsors "Paint the Town" days, during which thousands of volunteers paint

Above: Mayor Martin J. Chávez and his wife Margaret Aragón de Chávez.

Below: Community policing is among the Chávez administration's many innovations.

new Botanic Garden, Aquarium and Aquatic Park.

Albuquerque is also home to several museums of note. Historic Old Town is the site of the State of New Mexico's Natural History Museum and the Albuquerque Museum, which features art and local history; both facilities offer a number of special educational programs. A new museum combining science and technology awareness for children and youth will include a unique partnership with the Air Force's astronomical/cosmic research program to make the heavens available to the entire community.

Albuquerque is nationally renowned for its pioneering Open Space Program, in which more than 23,000 acres, maintained in natural form, are devoted to public recreation.

To meet the needs of its seniors, the city operates the Department of Senior Affairs, which furnishes a wide range of recreational and social services. In conjunction with Bernalillo County, the city also operates an excellent library system with 15 local branches.

A wide variety of plants are on display in the Botanic Garden.

over graffiti throughout the city.

—A water conservation campaign that encourages voluntary reduction of use, as well as strategies such as the use of xeriscaping and retro-fitting of water-efficient sprinklers in parks. Since the launch of the program in the spring of 1995, water use has decreased by 11%.

— A land use-design/transit-transportation strategy aimed at supporting a sustainable community.

—A collaborative approach to relations with neighboring Indian Pueblos, in which the heads of city departments and officials of the tribes share resources in dealing with mutual issues such as water usage and transportation.

Albuquerque is in the midst of several projects to enhance the quality of life for its residents. One is the Albuquerque Biological Park, which is built around the city's state-of-the-art zoo, and includes a

Albuquerque has achieved a national reputation for its extensive network of neighborhood associations. The city encourages this grassroots movement through its Office of Neighborhood Affairs—which works in cooperation with the more than 220 neighborhood associations to maintain a high quality of life.

"The future viability of cities," says Mayor Chávez, "will be based on safe, attractive neighborhoods, good schools, and clean air and water."

The City of Albuquerque believes its citizens deserve the best—and it prides itself on providing it.　　🔺

First State Bank

First State Bank, a New Mexico–based independent community bank, has taken off like a rocket.

In 1988, First State Bancorporation, the bank's parent holding company, was created to purchase First State Bank of Taos. That acquisition marked the beginning of an aggressive growth strategy; the company went on to acquire National Bank of Albuquerque and First Bank Santa Fe. First State has outperformed all initial expectations—in generating

Since 1989, First State Bancorporation has grown at an average rate of 20% per year, a result of its fundamental commitment to its individual and small- and medium-size business customers and its community.

deposits and loans, improving profitability, and diversifying its asset portfolio in each market it has entered. Since 1989, First State Bancorporation has grown at an average rate of 20% per year. It now has approximately 150 employees and commands more than $250 million in assets.

"One of our major objectives is to provide prompt, professional service to all of our customers," says Michael R. Stanford, President and CEO. "We are a locally managed company, which means we're not required to consult with someone in a main office in another state before making a decision."

This flexibility allows First State to offer highly personalized service, which First State considers one of the fundamental keys to its success serving small- and medium-size businesses as well as individuals. The company prides itself on providing consistently outstanding customer service, making good loans, maintaining low overhead and high productivity, and actively participating in local communities.

An aggressive loan policy, including offering loans through the Small Business Administration, has contributed significantly to First State's earnings. Approximately one quarter of the bank's loans are related to construction—loans which traditionally tend to be paid off quickly. Loaning money always involves risk, but First State has forged a reputation as a company that works hard but cooperatively to recover funds from bad loans. The Uniform Bank Performance Report states that First State does better than 73% of its peers in such efforts.

Another area in which First State excels is technology —not for the sake of technology, but wherever

First State offers both the personal touch of a small bank as well as the benefits of the most advanced technology.

and whenever it benefits the customer or raises the quality or range of services the bank can provide. As a smaller bank, says Stanford, "We can implement technological changes more easily than a larger organization can. This has allowed us to respond quickly to opportunities to improve our service capabilities. First State Bank has one of the most technologically advanced wide-area PC networks in northern New Mexico." This network gives bank employees quick and easy access to customer information, making any branch of the bank as capable of assisting customers as each customer's own branch.

A growing number of First State clientele are taking advantage of the bank's PC banking capabilities. These afford customers the ease of obtaining information about their loan and deposit accounts, initiating account transfers, communicating with bank personnel, and other activities via their personal computers. The bank also offers customers 24-hour telephone access to obtain account information, and is even implementing a check-imaging system for reporting canceled checks. This system will give customers the convenience of no longer having to deal with batches of canceled checks, and will also reduce the bank's postage costs.

"As a community bank," continues Stanford, "we devote much time and effort to supporting the neighborhoods in which we live and operate." First State contributes both time and money to organizations such as Habitat for Humanity, the University of New Mexico, Albuquerque Technical-Vocational Institute, and ACCION New Mexico. Bank officers and staff are encouraged to take active and visible roles in civic organizations and activities. This extensive community commitment earned First State a Community Reinvestment Act rating of "Outstanding" from the Federal Reserve, the highest rating awarded to banks. First State intends to remain involved in many activities that benefit New Mexicans.

The volatile business environment of the moment makes complacency unaffordable. What works today may not work tomorrow. Like other businesses, banks must keep abreast of advancing technology to remain competitive. By continually improving both its technological and human resources to better serve its customers, First State Bank is determined to remain a leader.

First State Bank now has 14 convenient branches:

ALBUQUERQUE
Carlisle Office (Carlisle & Constitution)—
1418 Carlisle NE, Albuquerque, NM 87110, 241-7534
Lomas Office (Lomas & 2nd St.)— 111 Lomas NW, Albuquerque, NM 87102, 241-7134

Montgomery Plaza Office (Montgomery & San Mateo)—5001 Montgomery NE, Albuquerque, NM 87109, 241-7680
Sycamore Plaza Office (Wyoming & Academy)—5620 Wyoming NE, Albuquerque, NM 87109, 241-7613
Journal Center Office (Jefferson & Paseo Del Norte)—7810 Jefferson NE, Albuquerque, NM 87109, 241-7600

RIO RANCHO
1781 Rio Rancho Blvd., Rio Rancho, NM 87124, 241-7592

PLACITAS
221 Hwy. 165, Suite 4, Placitas, NM 87043, 241-7530

LOS LUNAS
2421 Main St. SE,
Los Lunas, NM 87031,
865-7006

SANTA FE
San Mateo Office—
(St. Francis & San Mateo) 600 San Mateo
Santa Fe, NM 87502,
982-6000
Downtown Office—
201 Washington Ave.,
Santa Fe, NM 87501,
982-6050

TAOS
Main Office—120 West
Plaza, Taos, NM 87571,
758-6600
Southside Office—
1021 South Santa Fe Rd.,
Taos, NM 87571,
758-6671
Northside Office—
1520 Paseo del
Pueblo Norte,
El Prado, NM 87529,
758-6642

QUESTA
2433 North Highway
Rd., Questa, NM 87556,
758-6660

First State embodies the spirit of New Mexico right down to the Southwestern design of the interior of one of its branches.

Furr's Supermarkets Inc.

The familiar logo of Furr's Supermarkets — an eye-catching sunburst on a red background — has come to mean many things to New Mexicans.

For shoppers in a hurry, the thirteen Albuquerque stores are convenient locations to purchase fresh rotisserie chicken, a pizza or a ready-made Chinese meal, a 49¢ video rental. For families, Furr's Supermarkets offer a wide range of products. For the

Furr's has served its customers since 1904, and served them in many ways.

6,000 New Mexican and West Texan workers, it is an equal opportunity employer that offers an employee share-holder plan and career-growth opportunities. And for children around the state, it offers a number to call to get help with homework.

"Not only do we try to provide the most complete assortment of food products of the highest quality possible, but we have focused on becoming good citizens in the communities where we do business," says Buzz Doyle, Furr's COO and President. "We devote all of the resources we possibly can toward education. Among other programs, we have the 'Apples for Students Program,' in which we furnish computers to schools in exchange for Furr's receipts."

The focus on community betterment — which also involves a literacy program, a service that provides newspapers to schools, a homework help line and a "Stay-In-School" program to help kids get through high school — has earned the company great esteem. But the main reason Furr's customers keep coming back is quality.

"Furr's succeeds in servicing the customers the way they want to be serviced and this has positioned the company for growth," Doyle observes. Furr's recently added two new stores, remodeled thirteen and

has additional sites under development.

Knowing how important it is to families to have low food prices, Furr's has consistently made an effort to keep its reputation as a low price leader. While some stores lure shoppers with loss leaders, Furr's has created partnerships with a number of leading brands that make it possible to maintain low prices across the board. A Frequent Shopper Program offers additional checkout discounts on brand products and other benefits. And Albuquerque families have come to depend on this, allowing the company to build a broad base of loyal customers.

Furr's also offers special services and products. Most stores have a bank, and several are equipped with a post office and pharmacy. Imaging Centers that offer competitively priced one hour and overnight photo service have garnered shoppers as well. Furr's carries a wide variety of high quality, low cost items under

Above: The Furr's Emporium at Lomas and Tramway.

Below: Furr's makes shopping as convenient as possible

Furr's offers a
large selection
and low prices.

its own label. Many supermarkets offer their own in-house brands, but Furr's conducted blind taste tests that revealed consumers preferred their products.

But Doyle says that while adding services and positioning the company for growth are important, food quality and freshness remain the company's primary focus. Furr's Bakery Departments offer dozens of baked-from-scratch items, including custom made cakes for special occasions, tasty donuts that have earned a local reputation, as well as a variety of delicious fat–free products. Produce, meats and deli products are another area of focus Doyle says the company puts at the top of their agenda.

Walk through any Furr's and you'll find clear, bold signage to guide you, an enthusiastic staff and appealing displays. The well lit aisles are always clean, the choices many.

The sum of all this is that the company is prosper-ing enormously, with sales nearly topping one billion dollars.

The company, whose corporate headquarters are in Albuquerque, now has seventy stores in thirty cities and is very proud of its achievements. Furr's has served its customers since 1904, and served them in many ways. The company has donated over two million dollars to schools, churches and other New Mexico and West Texas organizations. Furr's and its employees and vendors also sponsor an annual golf tournament with proceeds going to various educational projects.

Furr's future looks as bright as its logo. "We hope to grow and provide good, quality jobs for many people and provide a good shopping experience for our customers," says Doyle. "Our strategy is simple: to be the best retail chain in the Southwest."

The Greater Albuquerque Chamber of Commerce

Albuquerque, like all growing cities, requires wise planning and guidance if it's to continue to prosper. The Greater Albuquerque Chamber of Commerce is doing everything possible to put the city on the right course.

The chamber has assumed the role of catalyst in effecting crucial changes concerning a variety of quality of life issues.

Founded in 1917 with fifteen volunteer members, the chamber was originally known as "The Commercial Club." As it has evolved over the years it has played a role in such landmark local developments as establishment of the International Sunport, the New Mexico State Fair, the Albuquerque Sports Stadium, Crime Stoppers, Sandia Peak Tramway and the immensely popular International Balloon Fiesta. With its current membership of some 2,700 firms, including many luminaries in the business community, a staff of twenty-one and a large, active group of volunteers, the chamber is a major force in the city. Its mission is to dedicate itself to meeting the needs of the Albuquerque metropolitan area through encouraging economic opportunity and an atmosphere conducive to business. Toward that end, the chamber serves as a resource and problem solver, a promoter of the business community and an advocate for the well-being of Albuquerque.

Establishing community partnerships between the city and key organizations like Kirtland Air Force Base, the University of New Mexico, Sandia National Laboratories/Lockheed Martin, and Albuquerque Technical Vocational Institute — and engendering programs and events to recognize and celebrate these partnerships, is one of the

chamber's highest priorities.

The chamber has also assumed the role of catalyst in effecting crucial changes concerning a variety of quality of life issues such as transportation, air and water quality, and land-use planning, as well as such difficult and complex problems as crime and gangs. By supporting numerous initiatives such as a Regional Transportation Authority, water conservation and management, and the intelligent development of

Above: Local experts share their knowledge of timely small business issues each week at the chamber's Curbstone Conferences.

Below: Some of the professional staff of the Albuquerque Chamber of Commerce.

Some of the chamber's other noteworthy efforts include providing international trade opportunities through its involvement in the Camino Real Economic Alliance and trade missions; designing a leadership curriculum to foster personal growth and leadership capabilities in Albuquerque youth; sponsoring the Blue Ribbon and Crystal Apple programs to recognize outstanding teachers and students; facilitating partnerships between businesses and schools through the Join-A-School program; and coordinating a college scholarship fund.

Entering the world of electronic commerce is another remarkable development. A chamber home page has been established on the World Wide Web (http://www.gacc.org/gacc). This on-line resource offers instant access to chamber publications, its calendar of events and a business information and matchmaking program.

(From left to right), Chairman Bob McCabe, President Terri L. Cole, Chairman-elect Jeffry Sterba.

Albuquerque's burgeoning West Side, the chamber is helping the city's leaders deal with their most pressing problems.

The solutions to these problems, the chamber has concluded, can be found by taking a regional rather than a local approach. Albuquerque and the surrounding region are growing at a faster rate than ever and their fates have become intertwined.

The chamber also acknowledges the necessity of emphasizing Albuquerque's distinct communities. "The future quality of our city is directly related to the viability of the unique communities within our city," writes Chairman of the Chamber Board and local architect Bob McCabe, AIA, in the 1995-1996 Business Plan. "We need to identify and enhance the unique qualities of these integrated communities."

It is an exciting time for Albuquerque and an exciting time for the chamber. "At no time in Albuquerque's history has it been more critical to plan for our future," states chamber President Terri Cole, CCE. "We need to make some important decisions as to who and what we want to be as a place to live, raise our families and to be in business."

As Albuquerque stands on the brink of the next millennium, and positions itself for an unprecedented era of growth and development, the Greater Albuquerque Chamber of Commerce endeavors to foster regional cooperation. In the words of Chairman-elect Jeffry Sterba, "Economic development, transportation and air quality issues do not stop at city or county borders."

H. Parnegg Realty

Service and professionalism are the defining characteristics of H. Parnegg Realty. Parnegg, founded in 1955, is Albuquerque's oldest residential/commercial real estate firm.

"This is a personal business," avers Peter Parnegg, the agency's President. "People rely on real estate agents as they do on doctors."

This has been the Parneggs' philosophy for decades. Back in 1955 Sid Hertzmark and Hannes Parnegg left

Albuquerque native Peter Parnegg trains his agents to be highly skilled, knowledgeable advisors, not sales people.

their mortgage banking jobs to form Hertzmark - Parnegg Realty, Inc., a two-man operation. They soon forged a reputation as Albuquerque's premier agency for fine homes. In 1970 Hertzmark - Parnegg was named the agency for La Luz, the prestigious townhouse project designed by internationally acclaimed architect Antoine Predock.

In 1978, Peter Parnegg became a real estate agent, working first with another agency and then with Hertzmark - Parnegg. Five years later he moved to Los Angeles, intent on making his mark as a musician. He met with some success there, but in 1987 he returned to Albuquerque, convinced that real estate was in fact his true calling. He assumed control of his father's agency, which then employed 18 agents and posted gross sales of $56 million. It has since grown to some 80 agents in four offices - Uptown, North Valley, East Mountain, Placitas - and has gross sales of several hundred million.

Parnegg believes that the most effective agents are highly experienced, possessing both technical knowledge of real estate and knowledge of their market. The average agent at H. Parnegg has been in real estate for ten years.

Above: Hannes and Peter Parnegg.

Below: Adobe homes of Pueblo design are plentiful in this area.

"People choose realtors because they know them and trust them," Parnegg says.

He's assembled a team of agents who work to satisfy their customers' needs. Clients expect real estate agents to serve as their "eyes and ears," knowing exactly what the client wants and knowing the market well enough to find it. This means having a knowledge of the quality of neighborhoods, schools, parks, and the like. "We're not

ments of selling a new home differ from those of previously owned homes. The two directors of Visions have a combined thirty years of experience exclusively in new home sales.

Though they dominate the local luxury home market, their average sales price is approximately a mere ten percent above the average price of homes sold in Albuquerque.

Since its inception, H. Parnegg has also been involved in commercial real estate, specializing in apartments, industrial, and corporate commercial sales. The agency has brokered or developed dozens of major properties.

Parnegg believes the key to his company's success is to hire the best people possible and let them do their jobs. To let them do the best job possible, H. Parnegg is eagerly adopting the advances of the information revolution. It has a site on the World Wide Web (http://www.hparnegg.com) which contains the text and

Another type of adobe-style architecture features a pitched metal roof.

sales people," Parnegg says. "We can give objective advice." Even if that advice is that the customer is better off not moving.

H. Parnegg is the only Realtor in town affiliated with Christie's Great Estates, the prestigious organization that brings buyers and sellers of distinctive homes together. They've been listed in the Who's Who of Luxury Real Estate. They are also a member of RELO International, an extensive network of more than 51,000 member brokers that exchange intercity referrals and information. For the last several years their per agent sales volume has been the best in Albuquerque and among the best in the country.

Seeing a need within his organization for a division dealing exclusively with luxury properties, Parnegg created Parnegg Fine Homes. The firm is also responsible for Albuquerque's first new homes division, Visions. Visions came about because the require-

photos of approximately 250 listings as well as helpful information about Albuquerque. Most of the company's agents employ laptop computers to instantly access information about properties and their clients. In fact, virtually every machine and program that can facilitate a transaction or enhance an agent's productivity is put to use.

A real estate agency, in Parnegg's opinion, should not only have a meaningful relationship with its clients, but with its community as well. Though he surrendered his musical aspirations, Parnegg has made his mark in the talk show business, hosting a real estate program on KOB AM which provides listeners with useful information. He especially believes in the importance of supporting education and is a founding trustee for the Middle School at High Desert.

Jaynes Corporation General Contractors

As their logo indicates, Jaynes is in the construction business. The company started as a concrete subcontractor in 1946 and evolved into a general contractor in 1971. Today, Jaynes is New Mexico's largest general contractor, with branch offices in Farmington, New Mexico and Las Vegas, Nevada. It has extensive experience in health care, institutional, retail, office, warehousing and manufacturing facilities. True to its origins, Jaynes is also New Mexico's

Jaynes, New Mexico's premier general contractor, not only constructs buildings, it solves customers' problems.

premier structural concrete specialist.

Unlike most general contractors that engage subcontractors to do the majority of their work, Jaynes possesses a large, highly skilled work force that performs a significant portion of the labor involved in each project. This enhances project management by ensuring greater control over quality and scheduling. Their management team has deservedly earned a hard-nosed reputation for accepting nothing less than what they expect from themselves, which is constant improvement.

"Our business is solving owner's problems related to facility needs...not just constructing buildings," declares J. Howard Mock, the company's Chairman and CEO.

Jaynes' strengths are its people, experience, training and leadership, which have resulted in dynamic growth and numerous achievements. It's one of New Mexico's largest privately owned firms and has been voted Most Admired Company four times by the businesses who constitute New Mexico's Private 100. Engineering News Record has ranked the firm in the Nation's Top 400 General Contractors since 1984. Jaynes was the recipient of the 1991 U.S. Senate Productivity Award and the first

winner of the National Associated General Contractor's Marvin M. Black Excellence in Partnering Award in 1993. The firm was named Contractor of the Year by the American Public Works Association in 1992 and the U.S. Army Corp of Engineers in 1993.

By 1971, Jaynes had become New Mexico's largest concrete subcontractor. The decision to become a general contractor was prompted by this success and a long term view of the business and marketplace. Since then, annual revenues have grown from $800,000 to more than $92 million. Today, nearly half of Jaynes' work is negotiated and a sizeable amount is repeat business from satisfied customers.

Success has been a result of Jaynes' competitiveness

Above: The Jaynes logo is seen at many structural concrete construction sites in New Mexico.

Below: The Robotics Manufacturing Science and Engineering Laboratory at Sandia National Laboratories is an example of Jaynes' work.

This success led to the formation of Jaynes' Employee Relations Committee which, soliciting the opinions of workers from all levels of the company, continues to produce valuable ideas.

Though bricks and mortar remain unchanged, communication and computer technologies have revolutionized the industry. Keeping abreast of these advances, Jaynes' management teams are on-line and able to immediately access centralized information files concerning any facet of a construction project. Having the vital information they need when they need it allows them to manage their projects in the best, most efficient manner possible.

Los Alamos National Bank is one of Jaynes' many projects.

and its initiatives to improve training and service standards in the areas of safety, jobsite production and project management. As a subcontractor, Jaynes understood the value of customer service; as a general contractor, the firm makes it one of their highest priorities, seeking to establish a lifetime relationship with every customer. Another way the company distinguishes itself from most other general contractors is by its Warranty Service Team, which deals exclusively with customer needs and concerns that arise after the completion of construction. The team resolves problems, answers questions on equipment operations, and suggests maintenance procedures to prolong the life of the building and equipment.

Jaynes' corporate philosophy is to view every issue as an opportunity. Skyrocketing insurance rates in the mid-eighties caused the company to reevaluate its safety program, resulting in changes which ultimately increased profitability. When asked for their input, field employees campaigned for a drug-free workplace and recommended numerous improvements. Their safety program now ranks in the nation's top ten percent of peer group contractors.

Jaynes is mindful and appreciative of the industry and communities in which they earn a living. From the top down, the company's employees are active in the Chamber of Commerce, The Associated General Contractors, Little League, the New Mexico Symphony Orchestra, Albuquerque Civic Light Opera Association, Kiwanis, and many others. Mock served as President of the Albuquerque Chamber of Commerce and has been actively involved at the highest leadership levels with the New Mexico and National Associated General Contractors during the past twenty years. Don Power, President and COO, has served on the board of directors for St. Joseph Healthcare Systems, the Great Southwest Council of the Boy Scouts of America and the Greater Albuquerque Chamber of Commerce. Richard Rice, Secretary and Treasurer, has chaired the Albuquerque Balloon Festival and has held positions at the executive leadership level of the National Construction Financial Management Association. These activities are Jaynes' way of thanking the construction industry and local community for fifty years of growth and success.

Lewinger Hamilton, Inc.

Lewinger Hamilton, Inc., is New Mexico's largest locally owned, full-service commercial real estate company. Through its Albuquerque offices, Lewinger Hamilton provides leasing, brokerage and property management services throughout the state. It also offers these services through its affiliates nationwide.

Lewinger Hamilton is a customer-driven commercial real estate company offering a full range of services.

A customer-driven organization, Lewinger Hamilton provides responsive, productive, and innovative real estate services to businesses, financial institutions, institutional investors, government agencies, and individuals. "The goal of all of our services is to help our customers reach their goals," emphasizes John R. Lewinger.

Chief Executive Officer John Lewinger directs LHI's sales and leasing activity and is a vital member of Albuquerque's business community. He has spearheaded the Coalition for Quality Growth, a group of local pro-active business leaders, in their efforts to bring about ongoing improvements in Albuquerque and the surrounding communities. He is the president of the award-winning New Mexico chapter of NAIOP (National Association of Industrial and Office Properties/The Forum for Commercial Real Estate) and was recognized as Member of the Year for 1995. Lewinger served as a representative to the Southwest American-Japan Conference, where he met with a dozen ranking members of Japan's business community. Through his participation in key business organizations, he has been an advocate for the commercial real estate industry at the local, national, and international levels.

The Lewinger Hamilton brokerage team numbers eighteen of Albuquerque's top commercial agents, six of whom are designated Certified Commercial Investment Members (CCIMs).

Each agent has been hand-picked for his or her ability to handle the complex and challenging demands of commercial real estate. Their excellent service earns high accolades from clients and customers. It is no surprise that Lewinger Hamilton associate brokers Jane Clarke, CCIM, and John M. Henderson, III, CCIM, received NAIOP/New Mexico's 1994 top awards for leasing and sales, respectively. NAIOP named associate broker Karen L. Hudson as New Mexico's top leasing broker for 1995.

Hudson initiated the Conejos Business Park, bringing together Albuquerque architect/developer Knight Seavey, AIA, local financing, and a unique mix of tenants to create a model industrial park. Lewinger Hamilton's clients and customers greatly respect the company's depth of knowledge in site selection and project development. Associate broker James Mocho

Above: Lewinger Hamilton's principals: John R. Lewinger, CEO (left), and John J. Hamilton, President.

Below: Conejos Business Park is a model industrial park.

The Lewinger Hamilton staff at City Centre, one of the many Uptown office properties the company manages.

played a vital role in the initiation and subsequent development of the San Pedro Creek Estates subdivision, a 26,000 acre eco-community in Albuquerque's east mountains.

John J. Hamilton, President of Lewinger Hamilton, oversees the operation of the Property Management divisions, for which he implements business plans, systems, and operations. Designated as an ACCREDITED MANAGEMENT ORGANIZATION® by the Institute of Real Estate Management®, Lewinger Hamilton manages some of New Mexico's most prestigious properties. Their portfolio includes office, retail, multi-family, and affordable housing properties for private and institutional owners.

Lewinger Hamilton is proud of the people who make up its Property Management organization. Their management staff is led by three Certified Property Managers® who are affiliated with the Institute of Real Estate Management®, and the International Council of Shopping Centers®.

Hamilton has encouraged the company's highly skilled professionals in their formation of work groups. Employees from all levels of the company, including staff from Lewinger Hamilton managed properties, work in teams which meet regularly to review procedures and productivity. The benefit of the team concept is most evident in the increased interaction between staff and associates and their greater contribution toward growing the company and participating in its success. The company supports continuing education for its employees and associates and utilizes current and evolving technologies. Lewinger Hamilton's use of computerized systems keeps the company at the forefront of New Mexico's commercial real estate community.

Lewinger Hamilton is a full-service organization offering the considerable expertise of its staff in areas including site selection, project development and construction management, due-diligence, remote management of properties, and tax protestation, to name a few. Committed to providing quality services in brokerage and property management, Lewinger Hamilton demonstrates that knowledge, experience, and teamwork are the cornerstones of success.

Lovelace Health Systems

L ovelace Health Systems was founded in 1922 by two physicians, both afflicted by tuberculosis and drawn to the arid high desert of New Mexico for its curative powers. Since that time, the name Lovelace has become synonymous with health care in New Mexico.

Headquartered in Albuquerque, Lovelace is owned by CIGNA HealthCare—which provides health, dental, life, and disability insurance to employer groups,

Lovelace operates on the principle that the highest level of quality health care ensures cost effectiveness.

and which is, with more than 40 HMOs in the U.S., one of the nation's largest managed-care networks. Lovelace itself is a nationally recognized regional health care organization and New Mexico's only comprehensive, fully integrated health care system, complete with a physician group practice, hospital, HMO, a network of primary and specialty clinics, and an extensive network of contracted providers and services. Its specialties include a comprehensive occupational medicine department, a highly specialized cardiology program, and a hospital-based cosmetic surgery center. It employs 2,800 physicians, nurses, allied health professionals, and support staff in New Mexico.

The Lovelace statewide network provides services to both members and non-members of the Lovelace Health Plan. The company's goal is to provide excellent, cost-effective, preventive, patient-centered care. The "patient-centered" orientation means that all Lovelace employees and resources, and the patient and patient's family, contribute to the high quality, personalized medical services.

"Health care is still a people business," says John Lucas, M.D., Lovelace's President and CEO. "And I think the greatest strength we have is the high quality of our staff."

There are nearly 300 physicians in 43 specialties in the Lovelace Group Practice, which, along with the contracted

Photo by: David Nufer

statewide network of physicians, give patients a broad choice of physicians.

The Lovelace Health Plan consists of an HMO and other managed-care products. The plan, founded in 1973, is the oldest in New Mexico and serves nearly 145,000 members and 700 employer groups—in government, private industry, and small businesses. The plan offers affordable premiums, prevention education, comprehensive coverage, and access to a full range of health services. More

Above: Extensive women's health services is one of the many specialties Lovelace provides.

Below: State-of-the-art medicine is practiced at Lovelace's trauma center, the only Level II center in the state.

money by reducing unnecessary procedures. Evaluations are based on the results of treatment, patient satisfaction, cost, and technical quality.

Guidelines are used to help eliminate unwanted variations and inefficiency, suggesting the most effective course of treatment for patients. Lovelace's statewide facilities are linked to the Albuquerque Medical Center via telemedicine technology. This system uses computers, video cameras, and phone lines to enable primary care physicians and patients in distant locations to display the patient's symptoms and consult with a specialist in Albuquerque. Shared Decision-Making, an interactive video program, allows patients to participate in their health care decisions via a customized, understandable program about their condition and various treatment options.

Southwestern flourishes are much in evidence in the spacious lobby of Lovelace's main facility.

than half of all New Mexicans who belong to an HMO belong to Lovelace.

Lovelace's system includes primary- and specialty-care centers in Albuquerque, Rio Rancho, Santa Fe, Espanola, Las Cruces, and Farmington. Care is also provided in several other New Mexico communities.

"We're a member of what's called the Six Clinic Group," says Lucas. The member clinics, which include the Mayo and Cleveland clinics, are considered to be the best in the country.

"By trying to achieve and maintain the highest level of quality," explains Gayle Adams, Vice President of CIGNA Lovelace sales, "we will also be cost effective." Quality and cost effectiveness, she firmly believes, go hand in hand.

Thus, Lovelace is committed to Total Quality Management. Its employees continuously strive to find better ways to meet the needs of patients. Extensive evaluations of patient care are the norm, and help tailor care to patients' needs and also save

tion and various treatment options.

Lovelace has always maintained a health care philosophy based on prevention. It's committed to improving the health of all New Mexicans by providing free or low cost public screenings, educational programs, and information services to both plan members and nonmembers. To encourage women to seek care early in their pregnancies, Lovelace has eliminated co-payments for maternity office visits and has several prenatal care programs for new mothers.

Lovelace also operates the Prematurity Prevention Program, an outreach effort in which physicians and nurses work with patients with high risk pregnancies to ensure that the mothers receive proper prenatal care and education. "We've cut our incidence rate of low birth weight babies in half," Lucas proudly states, "and our C-section rate is one of the lowest in the nation."

Norwest Bank New Mexico

Norwest New Mexico began as a small, single-branch, local bank in 1912 in Tularosa, New Mexico, with total assets of $34,000. Today, Norwest is a dominant presence throughout the state. It operates 71 locations in 38 communities, and boasts total assets exceeding $2 billion.

Each Norwest Bank facility is a complete financial center staffed by trained, caring professionals capable of providing a wide range of products and services.

Myra Sabine, Vice President, Business Banking, says, "Norwest Bank is on the leading edge of serving the small business community."

The goal of Norwest's highly diversified staff is to assist customers in meeting their day-to-day financial needs with greater convenience and ease, and to help those same customers and clients determine and achieve long-term financial objectives with increased confidence.

As part of the long-standing Norwest tradition, personnel are deeply committed to the communities in which they work. In Albuquerque, Norwest's staff is involved in the community and personally and professionally dedicated to improving the quality of life for its people. "Community involvement is an integral part of the Norwest Bank New Mexico corporate culture," explains Vice President/Community Relations Director Doris Rhodes. "Our employees are encouraged to participate in a variety of community activities. Senior bank officers and managers serve as board directors for many major organizations within Albuquerque and throughout the New Mexico region."

Community Banking President Roxanna Meyers serves on the board of directors for the American Cancer Society. Bob Jung, President of Business Banking, has served as chairman of the United Way cam-

paign for the United Way of Greater Albuquerque. Chairman of the Board and CEO Larry Willard serves on the Board of Regents of the University of New Mexico, Albuquerque Economic Development, the Albuquerque Community Foundation, the Albuquerque Chamber of Commerce, the Boy Scouts of America Great Southwest Council, the Industrial Training Board for the State of New Mexico, and the Western States School Banking Board.

Although Norwest has changed as it has grown

Above: Norwest's new Tijeras office.

Below: Larry Willard, Norwest's Chairman of the Board and CEO.

serving the small business community by using aggressive, new methods to service small business borrowers in a timely and cost-effective manner."

Norwest Bank New Mexico is proud to be a part of Norwest Corporation, a $71.4 billion financial services company providing banking, insurance, investments, mortgages, and consumer finance services nationwide. This alliance with a national parent allows Norwest New Mexico to distribute more and better products and services than most of its competitors, further benefitting its customers.

However, its affiliation with the nationwide network hasn't diminished its belief in or dedication to the smallest office in the Norwest operation. Norwest prides itself on being "still 100-percent committed to branch banking"—in particular, to a concept of branch banking based on the community banks of the past: small, neighborly institutions where the customer received the very best in personalized service and where relationships were built on personal

A group of Norwest employees enjoys the Albuquerque Balloon Fiesta.

through the years, the company's basic philosophy has remained the same: Local decision making—bringing sales and services decisions as close to the customer as possible—is a cornerstone of its success. Nowhere is this philosophy more apparent than in Norwest's performance in granting business loans. With this localized decision-making capability, Norwest manifests its dedication to the continued growth and prosperity of the Albuquerque area's small businesses. It also, of course, relies on the expertise of its approximately 20 cream-of-the-crop lending officers who average 18 years of major league experience.

According to Myra Sabine, Vice President, Business Banking, "Norwest Bank is on the leading edge of

contacts and mutual trust.

The greatest challenge the banking industry faces in the future is the certainty that rapid change will continue to occur on an ongoing basis. The people of Norwest view this constant change as an ally—a view the bank has maintained for the nearly 65 years it has been serving satisfied customers. Norwest sees its greatest opportunity in its proven ability to anticipate, prepare for, and manage this change, and to develop the appropriate culture and processes to respond rapidly to the changing needs of its customers. The people of Norwest Bank New Mexico have pledged to meet the challenge of continuing change with enthusiasm and confidence, ensuring that their customers will receive even greater benefits.

Roses Southwest Papers

They are living the American dream. In 1981 Roberto and Rose Marie Espat left their native Belize to make a home in Albuquerque. They brought with them great hope, considerable ambition, and entrepreneurial experience—virtues they employed in creating Roses Southwest Papers, the Duke City's only paper conversion company. This family owned business manufactures paper napkins, tissues, towels and

Roses' phenomenal success arises from the company's relentless "commitment to quality" and the "special attention" it gives to its customers—such as McDonald's and Burger King.

bags from 100% recycled paper, serving the commercial, industrial, and consumer markets. Roberto serves as President and CEO, Rose Marie as Vice President, and their son, Robert Jr., as Marketing Director.

The Espats owned a successful paper conversion company in Belize, but Roberto was concerned about the political and economic volatility of Central America. So, seeking greater stability, they moved here and immediately fell in love with the city. They were, however, strangers in a strange land where nothing came easily.

When they began Roses in 1984, business got off to a slow start. They had initially targeted the consumer market exclusively but found it inhospitable— already dominated by well established name brands. Consequently, they turned to the institutional market, where they soon began to make headway. The Espats' combination of hard work, experience, and determination proved an irresistible force. The degree of Roberto's commitment is apparent in his statement: "At the beginning of a business, one must eat, drink and sleep their company. You dream your work."

Roses' output continues to increase.

By the end of only its second year, Roses had turned a profit. And its growth since then has been nothing short of phenomenal. Beginning with 10 employees and producing only toilet paper and paper towels in a 20,000-square-foot facility, the company has grown to 50 employees, and expects to surge to 80 soon. The product line has grown to include a bag and napkin division, and the physical plant has expanded to 80,000 square feet (with another 20,000 to 40,000 square feet expected to be added in the near future).

In 1994, the company rang up an impressive $7 million in sales. Spurred by the additions to the product line, Roses registered $12 million 1995 and it expects such dramatic increases to continue. Understandably, Roses is consistently ranked on the Hispanic Business 500 list, and in 1990 the Albuquerque District of the Small Business Administration named Roberto Small Business Person of the Year.

Roses expects to produce 23 million rolls of bathroom tissue and 400 million bags this year for customers including McDonalds, Burger King, the

As for their sales to Mexico, NAFTA has helped "exponentially." Prior to the controversial trade agreement they did no business there. Now, however, Roses both purchases raw materials from and sells finished paper goods to Mexico.

"Our exposure and track record speaks for itself," Robert Jr. says by way of explaining their growth. "One of our greatest strengths is that we're a small business. We're able to keep a lower overhead than most large companies."

Lacking a large, ponderous bureaucracy, Roses' management is also able to make decisions quickly in response to customers' needs.

"Our greatest accomplishment is the growth we've

Paper stock is readied for conversion into a finished product.

General Services Administration, and wholesalers and distributors throughout the western United States and Mexico.

Even given its ambition, sweat, and past successes, one might still wonder how a small, unknown company like Roses managed to win over giants like McDonalds and Burger King. These successes, according to Robert Jr., result from the company's relentless "commitment to quality" and the "special attention" Roses gives to its customers. As Vice President, Rose Marie's several responsibilities include supervising the company's quality-control program to assure that the products meet the customers' high standards.

Roses' cost is also a factor, and here the Albuquerque location has proved a special boon. The company's low overhead and favorable shipping rates from the city allow them to deliver their top quality goods at highly attractive prices.

experienced since 1985," declares Robert Jr. "There's a great deal of satisfaction in being part of a growing company, a company that continues to get better."

The Espats make a point of contributing to their adopted city. With only 2% of their sales taking place in New Mexico, they bring revenue into the local economy.

"We provide a lot of charity in the form of products to various nonprofit organizations," Robert Jr. points out. Beneficiaries of the Espats' largess include Casa Angelica, Victory Outreach, and Joy Junction, among several others. Robert and his father also participate in such community organizations as Del Norte Rotary, Del Norte Rotoract, and ACCION.

The qualities that form the spirit of Roses Southwest Papers are the very ones that have formed our country. It should be no surprise that even here, in the high desert, Roses is flourishing.   🏭

Sivage Thomas Homes

What Michael Sivage, President of Sivage Thomas Homes, always keeps in mind is "why we're here and what we're trying to do." He need only think of his company's mission, which is "...to provide high quality homes in quality neighborhoods, with designs and features that meet the changing needs of today's families; to ensure an excellent investment for every buyer, and to do all of this at the most competitive price."

Sivage Thomas' commitment to quality ensures that its customers get the very best product at the very best price.

Michael's father, David, has been building homes in New Mexico for more than 30 years. David founded the company in 1985 as a joint venture with El Paso, Texas-based George Thomas Homes. The family moved to Albuquerque the following year. From it's inception, Sivage Thomas was a family operation. "Mom did the bookkeeping, Dad arranged the financing, I ran the construction," remembers Michael. By 1987, the Sivages had established themselves as the largest builder of single family homes in Albuquerque. They accomplished this by "offering customers what they were looking for." Sivage Thomas now employs 135 dedicated people—whom the founders consider members of a larger extended family.

Sivage Thomas builds homes to suit virtually every type of buyer. Their homes range in price from $80,000 to $300,000, and in size from 1,200 to 3,700 square feet. "We try to design a house to meet the buyer's needs," says Sivage— "and to deliver the best product they can get for the money." As a result, meticulous planning goes into every facet of a Sivage Thomas home.

Another of the many factors distinguishing Sivage Thomas from its competitors is its flair for innovative, exciting designs. Nationally renowned architects render imaginative, expansive, award-winning floor plans and beautiful exteriors. With more than 70 floor plans to choose from—and each plan offering several different options—the company offers a wide variety of designs to satisfy virtually any buyer's desire.

Being a builder/developer, Sivage Thomas does more than merely build homes. It develops communities. The best communities, says Michael Sivage, are those in which the builder is also the developer. As a developer, Sivage Thomas is able to purchase

Above: A proud sponsor of the Kodak© Albuquerque International Balloon Fiesta, Sivage Thomas boasts balloons as distinctive as their homes.

Below: Award-winning homes are a trademark of Sivage Thomas.

Their commitment to quality extends to choosing the best construction materials and working only with subcontractors who provide excellent products and services. The company also offers one of the best homeowner protection policies in the industry, guaranteeing the quality and superiority of the construction from the ground up—and a 10-year structural warranty.

The company's customer service department is available to assist home buyers in every way possible. "We continually work on the process of how to improve our product, how to improve our service," Sivage says. He hopes to make it possible for anyone in the company with a computer to immediately answer any questions customers have regarding their homes. It is this commitment, among other things, that has earned the company a Diamond Builder Award for Excellence in Customer Satisfaction.

"We take the same attitude with our employees that we do with our customers," says Sivage. The company recruits good people, pays them well, and gives them respect and the opportunity to voice their opinions. A company, he believes, is no more than the sum of its employees.

Having achieved great success in homebuilding, Sivage Thomas is now expanding into other fields, such as building apartment complexes and housing on Native American lands.

With its hard work and a devotion to its customers, the close-knit family operation has flourished, becoming New Mexico's largest privately- owned home builder. Outstanding value and an impeccable reputation come with every purchase of a new Sivage Thomas home. More than 2,700 satisfied customers can attest to this.

From the flow of sunlight through a thoughtfully placed window to the shape of a delicately crafted niche, exciting designs distinguish Sivage Thomas' homes.

land at wholesale rates, and then pass this discount on to the customer.

The company takes as much care in the planning, layout, and design of its neighborhoods as it does with each home it builds, traits that have brought its communities national acclaim. Found in the best locations in Albuquerque and Los Lunas, and characterized by ample lots in neighborhoods that inspire pride of ownership, each community is built with a distinct identity and concept in mind.

Sivage Thomas believes in including the customer as much as possible in the process of building the home, and buyers are invited to visit their home anytime during the construction process.

Sunwest Bank

Back in 1924, Albuquerque Trust and Savings Bank opened its doors. Over the years this institution evolved into one of Albuquerque's best known banks, Sunwest. Today, Sunwest Bank of Albuquerque, N.A. has over $2 billion in assets and 30 branches and motor bank locations throughout Albuquerque.

Sunwest combines the personal touch of a small town bank and the vast resources of a large institution.

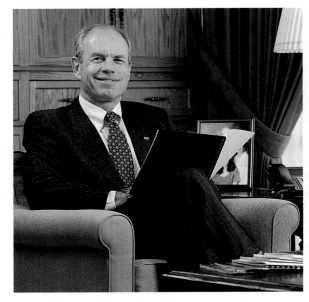

Sunwest is the flagship bank of Boatmen's Sunwest, Inc. (BSI). With $4 billion in assets and over 2,000 employees, BSI has the largest market share in New Mexico and ranks third in the El Paso, Texas market. Sunwest has over 75 banking locations, including community banks in Albuquerque, Clovis, Española, Farmington, Gallup, Hobbs, Las Cruces, Raton, Rio Rancho, Roswell, Santa Fe, Silver City, and El Paso. Each community bank has a president and board of directors made up of local business people and community leaders.

In 1992, Sunwest Banks merged with Boatmen's Bancshares, Inc. (BBI) of St. Louis, Missouri. BBI, with assets of more than $40 billion, is one of the 25 largest bank holding companies in the nation and the parent company of BSI. BBI has credit card, mortgage and insurance companies, and an investment services company, and ranks among the top providers of trust services in the country, handling assets of over $2 billion.

Since its inception, Sunwest has had a great impact in New Mexico. Bolstered by the Boatmen's merger, Sunwest combines the personal touch of a small town bank and the vast resources of a large institution.

"The dedication of our employees, the strength of our management team, and the exceptional service we provide to our customers combine to make Sunwest Bank the leader in the New Mexico market," emphasizes President and Chief Credit Officer Robert Goodman.

Sunwest offers a full range of personal and business banking services, including the largest automatic

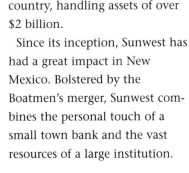

Above: Robert M. Goodman, Sunwest's President and Chief Credit Officer.

Below: Sunwest's senior executive management team.

institutions in the Southwest, it attracts the best and brightest employees, workers who are dedicated to the bank and its customers. Many of these employees have been on staff for more than a decade, and a good many of them for as long as 20, 30, even 40 years. This extensive experience, along with their professionalism, sincerity, and integrity, assure their customers' financial success.

Sunwest contributes thousands of dollars to hundreds of community organizations, considering it a responsibility and a privilege to give back to those who have contributed to the bank's success. Sunwest employees have a long tradition of supporting local communities, too. Their commitment to serving their customers is matched by their commitment to helping their neighbors and communities. The bank's officers and executives participate in nearly every community, civic, and charitable organization in the state, serving on boards of directors, task forces, and committees. Sunwest employees are leaders in local economic and community development efforts, working tirelessly to preserve this area's exceptional quality of life. Employees volunteer countless hours at numerous organizations, and through their energy and enthusiasm make Albuquerque and New Mexico a better place to live, work, and raise a family.

By combining the strength of a large banking organization, the personal service and attention of a local bank, and the strong commitment of its employees to their customers and communities, Sunwest Bank has earned its dominant position in the state and the loyalty of thousands of New Mexicans.

teller machine (ATM) network in the state with more than 200 Amigo ATM locations. The bank understands the financial needs of businesses, and their experienced loan officers provide financing for everything from commercial real estate to inventory acquisition. Businesses, large and small, benefit from the wide array of commercial services available at Sunwest.

The bank has the state's oldest full-service international banking department, which is staffed by experts who help companies conduct business anywhere in the world.

The Sunwest philosophy is to anticipate and fulfill customers' needs through the highest level of product quality and staff performance. Because Sunwest is one of the best known and most respected financial

The University of New Mexico Health Sciences Center

In July of 1994, all University of New Mexico health care facilities and programs were consolidated into a single entity named UNM Health Sciences Center (HSC)—the largest health care education, research, and patient care organization in the state. It represents almost half of the university's budget, has a staff and faculty of more than 6,000, and treats more than 120,000 patients yearly.

"By consolidating all of UNM's health related services under one umbrella organization," explains

UNM's Health Sciences Center brings together 12 agencies— including a top-10 medical school—to provide all of New Mexico with the best possible health care.

Jane E. Henney, M.D., UNM Vice President of Health Sciences, "we are positioned to better focus on the health needs of New Mexico. We're concentrating our efforts on providing New Mexicans with the absolute best educated and trained health care providers and most comprehensive services and still meet the challenge of conducting research."

Education:

The School of Medicine, created in the mid-1960s, boasts a wide array of nationally and internationally acclaimed programs. The M.D. degree program has earned the school international recognition, including consistent top-10 ranking in US News & World Report's annual listing.

The College of Nursing offers a bachelor's degree program to new students and to practicing registered nurses. Its innovative Distance Education Program allows students throughout New Mexico, southern Colorado, and eastern Arizona to earn B.S.N. degrees through interactive television course offerings.

The College of Pharmacy offers a Doctor of Pharmacy as the entry-level degree. The college is internationally known for its pioneer-

ing work in radio pharmaceuticals and also operates the New Mexico Poison Control Center.

The Health Sciences Library is the only comprehensive health sciences library in New Mexico.

Patient Care:

University Hospital is one of the state's major hospitals. The 372-bed acute tertiary care facility provides state-of-the-art patient care through inpatient, outpatient, and emergency services. University Hospital was recognized by the Health Care Insurance Association as one of the top 100 hospitals in 1994.

Children's Hospital of New Mexico, a part of University Hospital, provides the most advanced and comprehensive pediatric and neonatal care available

Above: The Health Sciences Center provides some of the most advanced health care in New Mexico.

Below: Having fun is part of children's healing process.

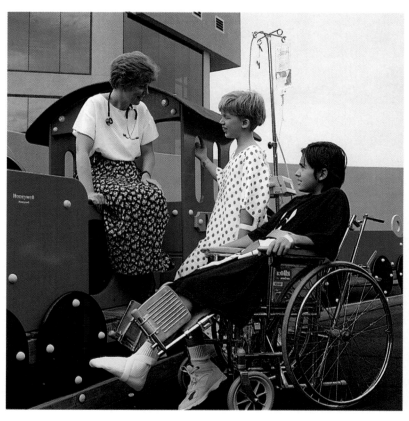

Research:

The Health Sciences Center is committed to strengthening its excellent research programs and expanding into new endeavors. New interdisciplinary grants include the National Institutes of Health-funded Geriatric Research and Education Center, a Robert Wood Johnson Foundation program to develop joint training for Physician's Assistants and Nurse Practitioners, and a grant from the Howard Hughes Foundation to support research infrastructure.

The School of Medicine is collaborating with Sandia National Laboratories on the development of non-invasive blood glucose and blood gas monitoring. The Cancer Research and Treatment Center has been highly successful in attracting research funding for molecular biology projects such as the identification of genes related to the development of adult leukemia.

Outreach:

"We continue to be committed to developing solutions for New Mexico's health problems through expanding our community service and health care throughout the state," says Henney. The HSC provides a vital support network that serves the needs of New Mexico's widely dispersed health care professionals; its faculty work in communities statewide, staffing regular outreach clinics, filling temporary vacancies, and providing consultations to community providers. Through the preceptor programs, students from the HSC are assigned to work with other health professionals in private practice, hospitals and community clinics.

Such a tremendous variety of services and accomplishments requires state-of-the-art technology and highly qualified staff and faculty. Meeting the health care needs of New Mexicans requires a strong interdependence of education, research, and patient care. These qualities make the Health Sciences Center a recognized source for a unique and comprehensive approach to health care.

The Health Sciences Center is known for its ground breaking research.

in New Mexico and the surrounding region.

Carrie Tingley Hospital cares for children with chronic physical impairments and developmental disabilities. It is widely known for orthopedic surgery, prosthetics/orthotics technology and fabrication, as well as rehabilitation services.

The Cancer Research and Treatment Center at UNM is devoted to cancer research, diagnosis, and care for patients throughout New Mexico and the U.S., and is the only such facility in New Mexico recognized by the National Cancer Institute. The CRTC has for twenty years been a designated center for compiling and tracking data on all cancer cases in the state.

UNM Mental Health Center provides inpatient and outpatient treatment for adults and adolescents. In addition, residential programs, the Rape Crisis Center and emergency services are available to residents of Bernalillo County.

The Children's Psychiatric Hospital provides intensive treatment for children ages 4 through 14 with serious psychiatric problems. This treatment takes place in residential settings or in a day-hospital facility.

Albuquerque Technical Vocational Institute

For three decades Albuquerque Technical Vocational Institute (TVI) has graduated students with the skills demanded by the employers who drive Albuquerque's economy. TVI has earned a stellar reputation by training expert bakers, nurses, accountants, and computer-chip technicians – the very heart of this city's dynamic work force.

For more than thirty years TVI has helped build Albuquerque's dynamic work force.

"Making people employable is TVI's mission," says Dr. Alex A. Sanchez, the school's President. "Education, especially job training, holds the key to personal and societal success."

Every year about one thousand people earn an occupational certificate or associate degree from TVI, 90% of whom find immediate employment in their fields. Thousands more improve their job prospects by taking one or more classes ranging from basic literacy to welding. Many others benefit from the custom training TVI provides at their job sites or by completing a self-paced exercise at one of the school's walk-in learning centers.

Success is one of the many subjects taught at TVI. Among the corporations continually taking advantage of the school's training are some of the city's best known: Baxter Healthcare, General Mills, General Electric, Motorola, Presbyterian Healthcare, Metropolitan Life, and the Rio Rancho plant of Intel Corporation.

TVI possesses such assets as a knowledgeable faculty who specialize in hands-on instruction, a thousand or more local employers who serve on advisory committees, and first-rate equipment such as advanced industrial

robots.

TVI is an accredited community college, offering certificates in 32 occupational fields, associate degrees in 27 occupational fields and the liberal arts, college transfer courses in 28 liberal arts disciplines and adult/developmental classes in such areas as English, math and GED preparation. Approximately 20,000 students attend classes on its four campuses: the Main Campus, near Downtown; the Joseph M. Montoya Campus, in the Northeast Heights; the Rio Rancho Campus, in the northwest area; and the South Valley Campus.

Since opening in 1965, TVI has promised "Education You Can Use." It has never failed to deliver.

Above: TVI's stylish Student Services Center.

Below: The lessons of high-tech are learned at TVI's robotics laboratory.

Arthur Andersen

Boasting more than 82,000 employees, 80,000 clients, and 361 offices, the Arthur Andersen Worldwide Organization is the world's largest public accounting and professional consulting firm. It is composed of two business units: Arthur Andersen LLP and Andersen Consulting. Arthur Andersen LLP provides accounting, auditing, tax, business, and other advisory services, while Andersen Consulting specializes in all aspects of systems integration.

To meet clients' most complex and specialized needs, local office personnel can call upon internationally recognized experts working throughout Arthur Andersen's worldwide organization.

When it opened in 1979, Arthur Andersen's Albuquerque office had one client. It has since become the largest and fastest growing accounting and consulting firm in the region. The office provides clients throughout the Southwest with accounting, audit, and tax services, and a variety of important, innovative advisory services such as state and local tax consulting, business plan development, merger and acquisition structuring, internal audits, and control reviews. "Our growth," says partner Brad Preber, who manages the company's Enterprise Group division, "is a tribute to our personnel, who have diligently served clients by meeting and exceeding their expectations."

Arthur Andersen's stated mission is "to help our clients succeed in the global marketplace by delivering value in everything we do." The company accomplishes this with top-caliber, well trained employees who cultivate long term relationships with clients in order to arrive at a complete understanding of their businesses. These fundamentals are complemented by a "Think Straight, Talk Straight" corporate culture and state-of-the-art technology.

To meet clients' most complex and specialized needs, the talents and expertise of local office personnel are supplemented by those of internationally recognized experts working throughout Arthur Andersen's worldwide organization who can be consulted on the latest trends, technologies, legislation, and practices of all major industries. The company's tremendous resources and proprietary products and technologies include the Global Best Practices™

knowledge base, which identifies successful practices used by industries throughout the world; the EXCEED™ client-service program, which surveys clients regarding their expectations, needs, and satisfaction with Arthur Andersen's services; and WinPROCESS™ productivity and business audit tools, which enable Arthur Andersen to evaluate a client's performance versus those of its competitors.

The Enterprise Group division serves emerging businesses, taking pride in developing cost-effective, practical solutions to entrepreneurs' problems.

"We're also proud of our contributions to the community," Preber declares. Arthur Andersen's Albuquerque employees are very involved in civic, community, and professional activities, participating in more than thirty nonprofit organizations. 𝐦

Arthur Andersen's Albuquerque management group.

Ballard & Ballard

What is great marketing? George and Irene Ballard believe it's "injecting" a product into the marketplace.

Ballard & Ballard Enterprises, Inc., is a trade show marketing and exposition company offering complete consulting, design, and production capabilities.

"There's no better place to find out what's going on in your market or your industry than a trade show," says George.

"People can enter the market of trade shows very inexpensively," adds Irene. "Major trade shows aren't the only places companies show their products.

George Ballard has received the nation's most prestigious trade show design and marketing awards.

Small doesn't mean second-rate." However, making the most of a trade show opportunity requires more than simply showing up. Even large, successful corporations who present regularly at trade shows don't necessarily market their products effectively there.

The Ballards can do as much or as little as a client needs: recommend the best shows for the client, prepare budgets and marketing and sales plans, select or design an exhibit for optimal results, and train staff to run it and close sales. George specializes in designing exhibits perfectly tailored to clients' products or lines, while Irene represents many lines of prefabricated portable exhibits, which Ballard & Ballard sell at factory-direct prices.

George all but pioneered this field, and has been working in it for nearly 30 years. He has designed two World's Fair exhibits and conducts Trade Show Exhibitor workshops nationwide. He's a former Western Region president of the Exhibit Designers & Producers' Association, and has won many of the industry's highest awards, including the Grand Focus from the International Exhibitors Association.

Among the Ballards' many satisfied clients are hundreds of international, national, and local companies including BASF Structural Materials, McDonnell Douglas Aircraft Corp., the University of New Mexico, and Sandia National Laboratories. But the Ballards are eager to help companies of all sizes (they moved to Albuquerque from San Diego more than five years ago, seeing New Mexico —and Albuquerque in particular—as "fertile ground" for small companies). George, for example, designed a

booth for Kabana, a local jewelry manufacturer who used the booth at New York's International Jeweler's Trade Show. Ballard & Ballard won a prestigious design award for the booth, but more importantly, Kabana's show sales increased by 70%.

Irene's credentials are equally impressive. She has more than sixteen years of experience in marketing, communications and trade show marketing with such companies as Honeywell and General Dynamics. She, too, has received a Grand Focus award.

Above: The Ballards have the expertise and experience to help companies large and small.

Below: Having won many of his profession's most coveted awards, George is recognized in Who's Who International.

Contact Paging

Some twenty-five years ago, in Texas, Jon Word and Vaughan Hancock teamed up in the Boy Scouts. Little could they have imagined they'd again be teamed, years later, in an ambitious endeavor to provide effective, economical communication throughout New Mexico.

Their company, Contact Paging, is the state's largest locally owned paging company and aims to be the

"The customer wants the best price, best coverage and exceptional value," says Vaughan Hancock, "and that is what Contact provides."

largest in the Denver, Dallas, Phoenix triangle. Contact expects to grow to 200-plus employees and generate revenues in excess of $28 million. Word serves as President, Hancock is Vice President and Chris Ritchie signed on as CFO in 1993. Recently Curtis Hubbard joined the team to run the company's operations in New Mexico and Southwestern Colorado.

"Our plans over the next five years are to expand our paging throughout the Southwestern and Central United States," Hancock explains. "This includes the smaller markets and rural areas that other paging companies ignore."

Though cellular phones have become commonplace, the paging industry continues to thrive. Word believes that people understand the importance of staying in touch, and his company's challenge is to prove that paging is the most effective way.

"Contact Paging is a customer driven company," says Hancock. "The customer wants the best price, best coverage and exceptional value and that's what Contact provides."

The company offers not only traditional paging services, but also advanced messaging services and wireless data. It provides alphatranscription paging,

the most advanced paging product available. Paging technology continues to advance. The alpha numeric pagers are capable of conveying a great deal of information, from traffic conditions on I-40 to stock market quotations. Contact also provides numeric display pagers, tone and voice paging, alpha transcription service, voice mail, communications consulting to small and large businesses, nationwide paging and 24 hour customer service.

Contact has spent millions of dollars improving its network and products. This area's mountainous terrain doesn't diminish the effectiveness of Contact's technology, which requires satellite dishes that continue to diminish in size, transmitters no bigger than a filing cabinet, and electrical and telephone lines.

"We are moving to a satellite network," observes Hancock. "What that allows us to do is provide an extremely reliable signal to more places we were unable to cover previously."

Above: Contact New Mexico has the tools that allow customers to stay in touch in today's fast paced world.

Below: Contact's officers: Chris Ritchie, CFO; Curtis Hubbard, Regional Manager; Vaughan Hancock, VP; Jon Word, President and CEO.

Dartmouth Street Gallery

Years ago, in a former life, John Cacciatore made a living selling motorcycles and bicycles. One day his company was sold and he received $500 in severance pay, just enough to purchase a sports coat, business cards and start an art gallery in his third floor apartment. So, in August of 1982, began

The art of Kozikowski and Bagley and the business savvy of Cacciatore are at the heart of Dartmouth Street's success.

Dartmouth Street Gallery.

Cacciatore, an art lover, now operates out of a comfortable space in the fashionable Nob Hill district, offering a mix of both traditional and abstract works by living New Mexico artists.

Numerous artists show at his gallery, but Cacciatore focuses on a core group which includes Nancy Kozikowski and James Bagley. He believes these artists are the equal of any.

"I think it's a combination of unique vision and technical virtuosity" that distinguishes Kozikowski and Bagley, explains Cacciatore.

"I think my work tends to be really strong whether it's figurative or abstract," Kozikowski, who also weaves tapestries, states. "You come into a room with my paintings and you can feel them in the room." Her art is at once new and familiar.

"I paint in a traditional style," says Bagley, a landscape painter. "I tend to want to paint not only what I see when I'm out there but also what I felt at that time." His work is enriched by a subtlety that allows the viewer to complete the painting.

Dartmouth Street's success results from Kozikowski and Bagley's art and Cacciatore's business acumen. Purchasing art has never been so easy. He makes

house and office calls, bringing art to the customer. Buyers can "test drive" a work, taking it home for a few days with no obligation, to be certain it suits their setting. Cacciatore handles commissions, offers a monthly payment plan and takes trade-ins. He also publishes catalogues of his artists' work, which are mailed throughout the country.

"Albuquerque is the art center of the universe," Cacciatore proudly declares. And Dartmouth Street Gallery is the fine arts center of Albuquerque.

Above: Another Day's End by James Bagley, 24" x 80" oil on canvas, 1995

Below: Tangled Belt #5 by Nancy Kozikowski, 48" x 48" wool tapestry, 1995

Envirco

Imagine, if you can, a particle 2,000 times smaller than a human hair. Or an air-filtration system so powerful that, of every 10,000 such particles that try to penetrate it, only three succeed.

Albuquerque-based Envirco manufactures just such products, serving the various highly-specialized needs

President and CEO David Schlegel encourages calculated risk-taking and innovation in the belief that his company has to "provide better products every day."

of the biotechnology, pharmaceutical, medical device, microelectronic, and health care markets—and of such well-known companies as Intel, Motorola, Eli Lilly, Texas Instruments, and UCLA Medical Center.

The idea for laminar flow clean rooms (areas in which the flow of purified air is completely controlled) was developed in the early 1960s by Willis Whitfield, an engineer at Sandia National Laboratories. Five years later, a prototype of Whitfield's concept was built by Comfortair, which began a clean-room manufacturing facility. Comfortair changed its name to Envirco in 1968 and the company has continued to expand clean air technology through product innovations and technical support services. In 1993, President and CEO David Schlegel and two partners purchased the company. The following year, Envirco's sales increased by 50%; they're expected to grow another 30% in 1995.

"We deal with very tightly controlled environments with very critical applications," Schlegel points out. "We control the air and we clean it."

To do that, Envirco manufactures 25 products—of which about half are patented, and a third of which are custom-engineered. The Hospi Gard, which they co-invented with the John Hopkins School of Hygiene and Public Health, is a portable filtration system designed to deal with the out-

Through outstanding research and development, Envirco is determined to stay ahead of its competition.

break of tuberculosis and airborne viruses such as Hanta and Legionnaire's Disease. The Enviramedic series is designed to purify hospital operating rooms, while the Biohazard Cabinet allows for safe viewing and handling of hazardous substances. And the company's patented Variable Air Volume/Bypass Filtration System is a revolutionary technology designed to both lower energy consumption and improve air quality in office buildings.

Envirco successfully competes against a number of national and international companies.

"Good people and strong incentives are the key," says Schlegel. "A lot of our employees have been here 15, 20, 25 years. We have a good research and development department, good innovation. You have to incentify people to take calculated risks." Especially since, Schlegel says, the greatest challenge Envirco faces is "to continue to innovate. I think you have to provide better products every day."

Eye Associates of New Mexico and Southwest Colorado, P.A.

Albuquerque has earned a reputation as a model health care center in part because of visionary, innovative organizations like Eye Associates of New Mexico and Southwest Colorado, PA. Eye Associates provides state-of-the-art care in ophthalmology and each of its sub-specialties, including refractive surgery, no-stitch cataract surgery, corneal and external disease, retinal and vitreous disorders, glaucoma, laser surgery, uveitis, oculoplastics, pediatric ophthalmology, and neuro-ophthalmology.

Eye Associates has become a benchmark in the industry because of its size and efficiency.

"We are the largest multi-specialty eye-care practice in the Southwest," says Carol Johnson, Director of Communications and Staff Relations.

A practice of four doctors when it formed in 1980 — Robert W. Reidy, MD, Arthur J. Weinstein, MD, R. Joe Cannon, MD, and the late Gerald S. Rubin, MD — Eye Associates now boasts a roster of six times that many physicians, working out of 15 offices in New Mexico and Colorado to serve patients from those states and also from Texas, Oklahoma, Utah and Arizona.

"We've become almost a benchmark in the industry because of our size and efficiency," says Johnson.

Eye Associates' prominence is due to its innovative practices. It's the only ophthalmological center in New Mexico and one of a mere handful nationwide chosen to participate in an investigational study of the Nidek excimer laser. The Nidek laser is being used in clinical trials to perform Photorefractive Keratectomy, or PRK. PRK can reshape the cornea to alter its refracting or light-bending powers, reducing nearsightedness. Eye Associates' Dr. Mark Lesher, who trained for a full year on use of the laser, is serv-ing as local supervisor of the trials.

The organization also broke new technological ground in 1994, when its surgeons performed the first automated lamellar keratoplasty (ALK) surgery in New Mexico, another treatment to correct severe nearsightedness. Eye Associates is still the only practice performing ALK in the state.

And, adds Johnson, "Two of our doctors were instrumental in designing surgical instruments and lens implants to coordinate with a new cataract removal technique."

But Eye Associates' concerns go much deeper than technology. In its ongoing effort to serve the community, the practice was one of the first in the Southwest to create a Total Quality Improvement Department to encourage every employee to strive continually for excellence. And as far back as 1984 it began offering free glaucoma screening clinics (the first in Albuquerque)—which it still offers one or two Saturdays a year. Eye Associates also conducts health fairs, visiting companies, schools, community centers, and senior centers throughout the area and providing free vision screenings.

Eye Associates' main clinic is Albuquerque's beautiful Regina Hall, built in 1912 and listed in the National Historic Register.

Flatow Moore Shaffer McCabe Inc.

Flatow Moore Shaffer McCabe Inc. (FMSM), one of New Mexico's largest architectural design firms, has a long, rich history, dating back to 1947. The company has attained its stature as a leading edge design firm through decades of experience in a wide variety of challenging architectural commissions.

FMSM provides a full range of multidisciplinary services to its clients, including architectural design,

FMSM possesses wide ranging expertise and experience in all types of architecture and designed environments.

interior design, urban design and master planning, as well as mechanical and electrical engineering. The company also provides construction management services. Computer animation and video services are provided by a division of FMSM, an exciting company named Virtual Animation System Management (VASM). VASM creates state-of-the-art computer animated walk-throughs of projects, allowing clients to virtually tour a building while it's in the design phase.

"We do significant work in the high-tech area with companies like Intel," states Bob McCabe, one of the firm's four principals and former Chairman of the Board of the Greater Albuquerque Chamber of Commerce.

When Intel first decided to open a New Mexico plant, it chose FMSM over numerous other firms to do a location analysis, which led to the selection of Intel's Rio Rancho site. FMSM was chosen because of its high tech expertise and knowledge of the middle Rio Grande region, and the firm has played an important role in providing design input into all of Intel's subsequent multibillion dollar expansions.

FMSM's commitment to technology as a design resource is exemplified by its home page on the World Wide Web (http://www.fmsm.com/fmsm/). By using tools such as the Internet, they're able to communicate instantly with clients and specialty consultants throughout the country.

"Our corporate mission is to bring quality to people's lives through visionary design," McCabe says. This mission has been realized locally, regionally, and at the national level for major clients such as the Marriott Corporation, Disney Development, Hilton Corporation, and NASA.

FMSM's dedication to visionary design, coupled with a sensitivity and understanding of this unique Southwestern region, has made this company a leader among its peers.

(From left to right) Bob McCabe, Principal; Jon Moore, President; Tobias Flatow, Principal; Rusty Shaffer, Principal.

Foods of New Mexico

Years ago, in his kitchen in the South Valley of Albuquerque, Larry Gutierrez perfected the art of transforming fresh ingredients into delicious New Mexican meals. He applied this expertise to a store of great family recipes and in 1975 opened Little Anita's restaurant.

Little Anita's caught on with diners hungry for superb New Mexican food, and the initial restaurant

Foods of New Mexico succeeds by providing both restaurant and supermarket customers with outstanding, authentic New Mexican food that is also convenient and affordable.

led to others (Gutierrez now operates four), and to Gutierrez' acquisition of the renowned Maria Teresa Restaurant, which offers standout Southwestern and Continental cuisine in the romantic ambiance of an 1840 hacienda in Albuquerque's Old Town.

So successful were the restaurants that Gutierrez eventually created Foods of New Mexico, a division manufacturing packaged entrees that are sold in supermarkets nationwide. Foods of New Mexico concentrates on being consistent, efficient, and extremely productive while maintaining the highest quality. In fact, the growth of both divisions can be attributed to providing restaurant and supermarket customers with authentic New Mexican food in the most convenient and affordable manner possible.

"The popularity of New Mexico has grown dramatically in the past fifteen years—as both a vacation destination and a style influence," points out Gutierrez. "A major aspect of the New Mexican experience is our very special cuisine."

Originally, the manufacturing division produced a single product. It now offers nearly twenty. Preparation involves chilling the food immediately after cooking—a technique that maximizes retention of flavor and texture.

The food is then packaged with a transparent plastic top to display its attractiveness.

Foods of New Mexico products were among the first entrees to be sold in a package which allowed for immediate preparation or refrigeration for up to ten days. They are the first and only company supplying ready-to-eat New Mexican entrees in this packaging in the country.

"By the year 2000," says Gutierrez, "we want to position ourselves to be an industry leader in providing quality New Mexican specialties for the entire country." Providing the highest quality food at the lowest possible prices requires imaginative, time-tested recipes and constant attention to the details of production and packaging.

Above: Delicious, ready-to-eat New Mexican entrees are Foods of New Mexico's specialty.

Below: Albuquerqueans have dined at Little Anita's for more than twenty years.

Intel

Intel Corporation, the largest single producer of computer chips in the world, opened its first New Mexico "fab" (fabrication plant) in Rio Rancho in 1982, and since then computer chips have become to Albuquerque what cars are to Detroit. Due to this area's good infrastructure, attractive tax incentives, a skilled work force and good technical schools, Intel has subsequently expanded this facility several times.

The Rio Rancho complex is the largest manufacturing site in Intel's worldwide operation.

In 1993, despite being furiously courted by other states, Intel initiated a $2 billion expansion of the site—and now expects to spend up to another $8 billion to retool its state-of-the-art manufacturing facilities in New Mexico. "Clearly, Intel is 'bullish' on doing business in New Mexico," says Bill Sheppard, the company's Site Manager.

The sprawling Rio Rancho complex—with 5,000 employees, Intel's largest manufacturing site—consists of three fabs manufacturing such products as the Pentium® and Pentium® Pro microprocessors and flash memory.

Various factors contribute to Intel's success. The corporate culture is open, aggressive, self critical, and highly focused. The company invests heavily in research and development (some $1 billion in 1995), and in technology at all levels of the manufacturing process.

Intel has also invested in safeguarding the environment. Since 1980, $260 million has been spent on environmental improvements including thermal oxidizers (which reduce volatile organic compound emissions by at least 90%) and water-use reduction efforts that will lead the company to conserve or recycle 39% of its water in 1996.

These investments have paid handsome dividends for New Mexico. Intel's payroll is approximately $250 million annually, with the average salary being $35,000—twice the state's per capita income. Approximately $120 million more is spent yearly purchasing local goods and services. Intel is also the largest payer of corporate income taxes in New Mexico.

Intel has assumed the role of community benefactor as well. It has established collaborative partnerships with several schools, Sandia and Los Alamos National Laboratories, and many civic organizations to achieve common goals—among them a "school-to-work highway" that expeditiously transports students from the classroom to good jobs. Intel has donated computers, trained teachers, granted internships to students, and in 1995 pledged to contribute $30 million to the building of a high school for Rio Rancho's new independent school district.

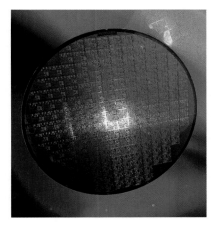

Above: A Pentium® processor wafer with 133 MHz chips.

Below: At Intel's Visitor Center, high school students learn about the world of high-tech.

Interamerica Bank

In February of 1995, Albuquerque's impressive financial community was made more so with the addition of Interamerica Bank, conveniently located at 2400 Louisiana NE—across from Coronado Mall in uptown.

Interamerica is one of America's few Mexican-owned banks. International banking is its proven forte, and it's capitalizing on the tremendous trade

Interamerica is a proven leader in international banking, but also boasts the flexibility of a community bank, offering consumer, business, commercial real estate, and various SBA loan programs.

and investment opportunities created by the North American Free Trade Agreement (NAFTA).

"We're ready to serve the foreign banking needs of the community," declares Interamerica Chairman Ruben Rodriguez Quezada.

Interamerica's bilingual staff has considerable experience and expertise in international trade and investment. These skills, plus the bank's foreign contacts—especially in Mexico—provide invaluable assistance in arranging trade and project financing and helping U.S. businesses gain entry into foreign markets. Interamerica's capabilities are especially helpful in aiding its customers in such critical matters as the documentation, credit, and legal complexities often encountered in international transactions.

Exporting, importing, foreign investment, joint ventures both in the U.S. and abroad—these are all vital to the growth of this region. Interamerica Bank is superbly positioned to help New Mexico businesses and individuals as they expand into world markets.

But Interamerica excels in more than international banking. It also boasts the flexibility of a small, community bank.

"We have an active and growing commercial loan department, specializing in servicing small and medium sized businesses," Rodriguez Quezada observes. Their highly experienced loan officers are very familiar with the local market and offer personalized

and innovative solutions to their customers' needs.

Interamerica's many customers also appreciate the bank's personal approach to business. Every account is handled here in Albuquerque, and the bank's officers are always readily available.

Interamerica is proud to contribute to the progress and growth of the region. Through membership in the Albuquerque and Hispano Chambers of Commerce and participation in the various New Mexico Economic Development Department programs, the bank is actively promoting local and regional businesses. In an increasingly international business climate, Interamerica Bank is uniquely suited to serve the area's present and future banking needs.

Above: Interamerica has made its presence felt in the financial community.

Below: Ruben Rodriquez Quezada, Chairman, brings experience in international finance to Interamerica.

New Mexico Heart Institute

In 1994, Cardiology Associates of New Mexico and the New Mexico Heart Clinic (NMHI) merged with Cardiac Surgery of New Mexico to form the New Mexico Heart Institute, the largest cardiovascular group in the state. NMHI provides comprehensive cardiovascular services to patients throughout the Southwest at its five clinics in Albuquerque, clinics in

New Mexico Heart Institute's mission is to provide world–class cardiovascular care.

Santa Fe and Roswell, and twenty other facilities in communities in New Mexico, Colorado and Arizona.

The merger brought a wealth of experience under one roof, including specialists and their support staff in the fields of preventive and interventional cardiology, interventional electrophysiology, nuclear medicine, echocardiography, congestive heart failure, and cardiovascular surgery, including transplantation. NMHI's excellence was recognized by the Cardiology Preeminence Roundtable 1995 which, choosing from private cardiovascular groups throughout the United States, identified NMHI as one of five outstanding providers of quality patient care.

NMHI's mission focuses on the four cornerstones of patient care, prevention, education, and research to achieve its ambition of being a center for world-class cardiovascular care. Many New Mexicans have benefited from this expertise. NMHI is the oldest continuous provider of cardiovascular surgical services in the state and has performed more than 14,000 adult and pediatric surgical procedures since 1981, with results which consistently meet or exceed national standards of excellence. Their pediatric cardiovascular surgeons also donate their services and time to support a nationwide organization called Healing the Children. This group brings children from around the world to

Above: A technician takes an echocardiagram at the NMHI's echolab. This is an ultrasound procedure which makes an image of the heart.

Below: NMHI cardiologist Dr. Barry Ramo (who also serves as the medical reporter for KOAT 7 TV) performs a catheterization procedure.

the U.S. to receive medical care that's not available in their native countries.

NMHI is committted to education. Doctors and staff regularly conduct seminars for medical professionals, participate in continuing education programs, and, believing that knowledge is often the key to good health, educate patients and the general public. A unique feature of the institute is its Clinical Research department. NMHI physicians have coordinated over sixty clinical research studies since its beginnings in 1987, furthering understanding of cardiovascular illness, and advancing medical and surgical treatment for heart disease globally.

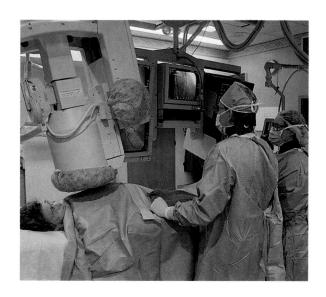

New Mexico Technet

New Mexico Technet, Inc., created in 1984, is a private, nonprofit corporation that manages a statewide fiber optic computer network serving the needs of the state, various research, educational, and economic development organizations, and the private sector.

Technet has been the primary Internet access provider in the state since 1985 and has the only

Technet has been New Mexico's primary Internet access provider since 1985 and offers an array of services.

commercial 45 mb connection. It directly connects over 200 schools and businesses as well as approximately 80% of the Internet service providers to the Internet. It offers an array of Internet access services from modem dial-in to direct connections, including full World Wide Web publishing and management services.

New Mexico Technet is a leader in providing access to public information files. A significant number of state, county, and local government databases are online to assist businesses in their daily operations. Some examples are:

— Insurance companies and agencies can review drivers' license records to assess their risk when issuing auto policies.

— Automobile dealers can register vehicles they sell directly from their dealerships.

— State tax forms can be filed electronically.

— Companies and individuals can access the Technology Transfer, Commerce Business Daily, and New Mexico Procurement databases, and the various state university databases.

— Attorneys can access U.S. and New Mexico State Supreme Court dockets and opinions, and obtain legal information from the University of New Mexico Law School Library and the State Corporate Commission databases.

Technet supports itself through user fees. These revenues have allowed the network to expand to meet demand and serve the community in many other ways. A third of Technet's gross revenues support education and economic development projects in the state. Among the many projects are:

— The New Mexico Super Computer Challenge - Over 700 New Mexico high school students compete for scholarships and computer equipment for their schools by designing and completing projects using super-computers at New Mexico's national laboratories.

— NEDCOMM - the New Mexico Educators Communication Network, which offers the Internet to teachers as a resource tool.

— DONORNET - Hospitals throughout the state can electronically register human organs donated for transplants with the New Mexico Donor Association.

In these and other ways New Mexico Technet has established itself as a national leader in improving commercial and educational opportunities through use of the Internet and connected networks.

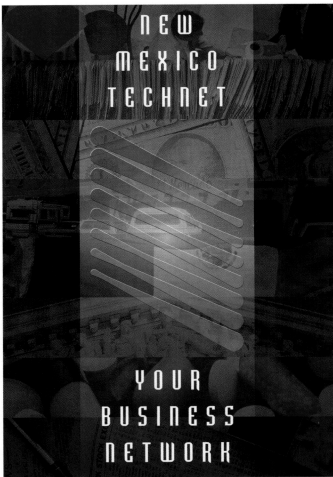

Technet provides an immense variety of information.

Public Service Company of New Mexico

Public Service Company of New Mexico (PNM) is a combined electric and gas utility serving a population of 1.2 million in more than one hundred communities around the state. PNM is organized into four strategic business units, each focused on a particular segment of the company's core business. PNM serves 333,000 electric customers and 393,000 gas customers through its Electric Services and Gas Services business units. The company's Bulk Power Services manages transmission and generating systems and sells power on the wholesale market. PNM

PNM is committed to providing the quality, reliability and convenience its customers have come to expect.

Energy Services operates the Santa Fe municipal water system and offers energy, water and waste water management, and energy conservation assistance to government agencies as well as to commercial and industrial customers.

PNM's business plan is focused on three strategic goals: strengthening the company's financial position, taking advantage of opportunities for growth in the evolving energy marketplace, and cooperating with all interested parties in shaping the future of the energy industry to the benefit of all customers and investors.

PNM President and CEO Ben Montoya says each of the steps the company is taking advances PNM's VISION 2000. "We intend to be a stand alone, competitive, investment grade energy services company and the preferred provider of energy services in the Southwest."

The number of PNM customers per employee — a key measure of a utility's efficiency — has grown from 207 in 1991 to more than 270. This increased productivity has resulted in lower prices for customers. In 1995, PNM was allowed to combine electric and gas customer services, which improved convenience for its customers and saved the company $1.4 million. Additional savings resulted from revising the procedures for connecting new customers. But realizing value isn't a function of price alone, PNM is committed to providing the quality, reliability, and convenience its customers have come to expect. It has, for example, installed a sophisticated computer system to better anticipate system faults

and respond more quickly to power outages.

With nearly 80 years in the energy business, PNM has the experience and the dedication customers can rely on.

Above: PNM utilizes sophisticated technology to offer its customers reliable, reasonably priced energy.

Below: PNM serves more than 700,000 customers.

Science and Technology Park at UNM

As its name suggests, the Science and Technology Park at the University of New Mexico is dedicated to the development and commercialization of technology. The park is a master-planned, 153-acre business and technology development with more than 360,000 square feet of office and research space existing or under construction. The park is adjacent to both I-25 and the university's main campus, and is

"We enjoy a unique atmosphere and perspective in the park — collaborative and congenial, but intense."
—Chuck Wellborn, President of Science & Technology Corporation @ UNM

less than a mile from Albuquerque International Sunport.

One of the premier research centers in the region—which is itself one of the premier research centers in the world—the park combines an immense array of sophisticated research and development facilities and office buildings in a beautiful, campus-like environment that encourages collaboration.

This collaborative atmosphere is already in evidence in the variety of activities being conducted here by components of UNM (a nationally recognized research institution, with almost $170 million in outside-funded research last year), Sandia National Laboratories, Los Alamos National Laboratory, and the Air Force's Phillips Laboratory. Other tenants include the Energy and Environment Sector of Lockheed Martin Corporation, Sandia National Laboratories Technology Transfer and Commercialization Center and other Sandia activities, and Albuquerque Technical Vocational Institute. Also housed here is the Research Institute for Assistive and Training Technologies, Albuquerque Economic Development, Inc., the New Mexico Engineering Research Institute, and the Alliance for Transportation Research, a multi-disciplinary research effort covering a variety of transportation issues, funded by many states and several foreign countries.

"We enjoy a unique atmosphere and perspective in the park," says Chuck Wellborn, President of Science & Technology Corporation @ UNM, which manages the facility. "It's collaborative and congenial, but it's intense. With the caliber of people and facilities available in the park and fiberoptic connections a standard amenity, nothing is beyond our capabilities." Major projects are currently underway at the park in the fields of electronics and microelectronics, photonics and optoelectronics, advanced materials, and space technology.

Significant additions, such as a $14 million, 59,645-square-foot Optoelectronics Center, and a 50,000-square-foot Manufacturing Technology and Training Center, are forthcoming. The Park offers ground and office leases and build-to-suit opportunities.

Above: The most sophisticated research is an everyday occurrence at Science and Technology Park.

Below: Science and Technology Park is a magnet for hi-tech organizations.

Starlight Publishing

In 1986, Starlight Publishing debuted with a single magazine, Albuquerque Living. It has since grown so dramatically as to become one of New Mexico's leading magazine publishing companies.

Starlight publishes *Albuquerque Monthly,* the *Santa Fean, New Mexico Business Weekly,* and numerous other guides, directories, and programs. The company has more than 40 employees in offices in Albuquerque and Santa Fe, and numerous clients in New Mexico, California and Colorado.

One of Starlight's primary ambitions is to keep pace with Albuquerque's growth and continue to make a significant contribution to the community.

Much of the growth has occurred because of the company's ability to generate new business. "We're extremely entrepreneurial," says Rick Homans, Starlight's Chairman and CEO.

Starlight has won numerous awards for its publications, including six Maggies from the Western Publications Association, one ADDY from the New Mexico Advertising Federation, and one Ozzie, a national award bestowed by Cowles Business Media.

"Our company prides itself on not only being one of the primary publishers in the area, but also on the fact that we are involved with the community we serve," explains Lyndell F. Gooch, President and COO. He, like Homans, is active in various community organizations.

Starlight's roster of publications is impressive and extensive. *Albuquerque Monthly* and the *Santa Fean* cover the politics, personalities, arts, dining, culture, homes and other aspects of these cities. The *New Mexico Business Weekly* is a statewide newspaper that focuses on hard news, profiles, business developments and other business topics. The *New Mexico Almanac* is an annual hard

cover publication filled with information about New Mexico and distributed in 10,000 hotel rooms throughout the state. Visitors and newcomers, through Starlight's several guides, become familiar with such cities as Albuquerque, Santa Fe, Rio Rancho, and Santa Monica, California. Design Studio is Starlight's design and production division. It produces ads, brochures, sales kits, direct mail pieces, corporate stationery packages, invitations, flyers, and logos.

"We're a cutting-edge company in terms of technology," Homans avers. He points to the company's use of the latest production methods as well as its page on the World Wide Web.

One of Starlight's primary ambitions is to keep pace with Albuquerque's growth and continue to make a significant contribution to the community. In pursuing this goal, it relies on the knowledge and experience of its board of directors which, in addition to Homans and Gooch, consists of Timothy G. Cockshutt, Hans H. Estin, Luther H. Hodges Jr. and Thomas H. Bonafair.

Starlight's principals Lyndell F. Gooch and Rick Homans.

The University of New Mexico

Created in 1889, the University of New Mexico first opened its doors in June 1892, with an enrollment of 25 students. One hundred and four years later, enrollment has reached 24,431 students on UNM's main campus alone—with another 6,499 students enrolled at the university's three branch campuses, two graduate centers, and the Taos Education Center.

In recent years, research, instruction, and public service awards to the university have increased dramatically.

At UNM, excellence in teaching is the norm, academic standards are consistently rising, and pioneering research is virtually always in progress. "UNM is currently involved in many activities that are strengthening our stature as a leading research university," says President Richard E. Peck. The Board of Regents has set the school the ambitious goal of becoming one of the top 25 public research universities in the nation—and of joining the elite American Association of Universities.

It is well on its way. UNM offers more than 4,000 courses, its libraries contain nearly 2 million volumes, and computer links provide access to nearly every other university in North America, as well as to major universities and research centers around the world. The university has a long-standing reputation of academic excellence in a number of disciplines, including biology, fine arts, anthropology, and Latin American Studies. And U.S. News and World Report has repeatedly recognized the School of Medicine as one of the top 10 medical schools for primary care in the country.

A wide variety of research is taking place, ranging in subjects from supercomputing and alcoholism treatment to reintroducing the Mexican wolf into the wilds.

Meanwhile, the university's faculty represents an exceptionally diverse range of academic disciplines. Efforts to recruit nationally-

Photo courtesy of UNM

renowned instructors have brought Nobel Laureate Murray Gell-Mann to the Department of Physics and Astronomy, and National Academy of Sciences member Jane Buikstra to the Department of Anthropology. The faculty is diverse in gender and ethnicity, as well; in fiscal 1994-95, some 48.8% of the newly hired junior faculty were women and 8.4% were Hispanic—rates well above the national average.

For academic year 1994-95, sponsored research, instruction, and public-service awards to the university totaled $182 million—a 10% increase over the previous year. The university is constructing a $14 million Optoelectronics Material Center at University Research Park, a $6 million Cancer Research Center, and a $9 million manufacturing and training center. A $300,000 grant from the Keck Foundation will soon result in an ultra–high resolution optical and x-ray imaging laboratory. The university also boasts a number of endowed chairs and professorships.

Photo courtesy of UNM

Above: UNM is known for its pueblo style architecture.

Below: The pond in the center of campus attracts both students and water fowl.

UNM Mesa del Sol

Welcome to a community where neighborhoods and open spaces, retail shops and services, industries and other major commercial entities don't merely coexist—they flourish. Welcome to Mesa del Sol, an ambitious, sensibly and sensitively planned, 13,000-acre community minutes from

When complete, Mesa del Sol, almost a city within a city, will be the most livable, innovative, and remarkable community New Mexico has known.

downtown, adjacent to major transportation routes, and ideal for industrial, commercial, and residential development. When it is built, it will be the most livable, innovative, and remarkable community New Mexico has known.

"Our goal," says Ray Powell, Commissioner of Public Lands, "is not simply to build housing but to build communities." Consequently, Mesa del Sol's buildings will be of human scale, public transportation accessible, commercial districts conveniently located. A network of trails will serve for both recreation and transportation. Street crossings will be pedestrian friendly. A sense of neighborhood will be strongly emphasized.

"This is an excellent location for businesses whose mission is related to Sandia and Kirtland," points out Harry Relkin, Assistant Commissioner. Kirtland Air Force Base and Sandia National Laboratories, which lie immediately north and east, have been offered parts of Mesa del Sol for purposes such as offices, research and development, and housing.

The federal government granted the lands that constitute Mesa del Sol to New Mexico when it attained statehood in 1912. The land is held in trust for the University of New Mexico and the state public schools, and administered by Powell. A native of Albuquerque, Powell is committed to Mesa del Sol's success. All of the property is within the Albuquerque city limits and will be serviced by the city.

"This is the kind of community that has proved attractive to large employers," says Tom Leatherwood, Public Lands' Planner—especially with the kind of dynamic economic growth the Albuquerque area is now enjoying. The State Land Office welcomes offers from joint-venture partners to participate in the visionary development of Mesa del Sol. Partners will be involved in everything from pre-planning to construction.

This vast, beautiful tract of land is perfectly situated for both business and residential development.

PETROGLYPHS ARE THE ANCIENT WORKS OF ART CREATED BY THE AREA'S FIRST RESIDENTS. THE DRAWINGS AND PICTOGRAPHS WERE PECKED WITH SHARPENED ROCKS INTO THE SURFACES OF BIGGER ROCKS. SOME 15,000 OF THESE PETROGLYPHS EXIST IN THE VOLCANIC ESCARPMENT OF THE CITY'S WEST MESA, BOTH WITHIN AND WITHOUT THE BOUNDARIES OF PETROGLYPH NATIONAL MONUMENT THERE. THESE FORM ONE OF THE WORLD'S LARGEST CONCENTRATIONS OF PREHISTORIC ROCK ART ADJACENT TO AN URBAN AREA.